An Illustrated History of

Lynton and Lynmouth

1770-1914

An Illustrated History of
Lynton and Lynmouth
1770-1914

John Travis

JOHN TRAVIS

Breedon Books
Publishing Company
Derby

Dedication

To the people of Lynton and Lynmouth,
past, present and future.

First published in Great Britain by
The Breedon Books Publishing Company Limited
44 Friar Gate, Derby, DE1 1DA.
1995

ISBN 1 85983 023 4

Printed and bound by Butler & Tanner, Frome, Somerset.
Cover printed by Premier Print, Nottingham.

Contents

Acknowledgements 6

Introduction 7

A Series of Disasters 8

The First Tourists 14

Early Road Travel 23

Sea Travel 32

Smuggling 37

The Revel 43

Conflict 45

Harbour Disputes 51

Personalities 60

A Glut of Schools and Churches 75

'The Healthiest Spot in the Country' 88

George Newnes 96

The Cliff Railway 108

New Lamps for Old 117

Boom and Bust 119

The Coming of the Railway 134

Pressure for a Pier 147

Shipwrecks and Lifeboats 152

Recreations 161

Motor Cars and Charabancs 176

Suggested Reading 185

Index 186

Acknowledgements

My first thanks must go to the many people of Lynton and Lynmouth who have given me help, information and encouragement while I have been writing this book.

I am deeply grateful to the librarians, archivists and curators of many institutions. Particular thanks must go to Les Franklin of the North Devon Athenaeum, Andrew White of the Lyn and Exmoor Museum and Sheila Stirling of the Devon and Exeter Institution.

I should also like to thank Phyllida Ovenden for information about her grandfather Sir Thomas Hewitt, Paul Gower for his enthusiastic help, Ann Wright for putting me on to a new source, John Loveless for his excellent work processing my photographs and Bill Pryor for his photocopying and interest.

I owe a particular debt to Andrew Farmer, Harriet Bridle, Derek Bishop and members of my family for reading my manuscript and making constructive suggestions for its improvement. Andrew Farmer also gave me invaluable assistance in dating my illustrations.

Most of all, I am grateful to Gwyneth, my wife, for her support and practical help. I would not have been able to write this book without her.

Illustration Acknowledgements

Special thanks are due to the following people and institutions for granting permission to reproduce illustrations in the book:

Derek and Hazel Blight: 100; Harriet Bridle: 10 (bottom), 61 (bottom), 66 (left); Marian Chubb: 73 (top), 85, 110 (top), 129 (top), 169 (bottom), 178; Ned Darch: 37, 95 (bottom), 104, 122 (top), 172 (top left); Devon and Exeter Institution: 16, 17, 18, 19, 20 (middle), 22, 24 (top), 24 (bottom), 32, 45, 49 (right), 61 (top), 66 (right), 91, 163 (bottom); Andrew Farmer: 40, 50, 52 (top), 75, 89 (right), 103, 120 (bottom), 123 (bottom); Roger Ferrar: cover (front bottom right), cover (back top), 25 (right), 44, 72 (bottom), 79, 121, 122 (bottom), 144; Molly Friend: 125 (bottom), 171; Paul Gower: 27, 34, 82, 84 (top), 86 (top), 86 (bottom). 101, 112, 115, 116 (right), 127, 128, 137 (bottom), 138, 148, 156, 172 (bottom left),. 173 (bottom), 175 (bottom), 176, 177, 181 (bottom); Gladys Harper-Buttle: 170 (right); Flo Hildick: 169 (top); Ilfracombe Museum: 26 (bottom), 33, 136; Edna Jewell: cover (front bottom left), 137 (top), 183; Knights Photographers: 141 (top); Trevor Ley: 111 (top); John Loveless 51 (right), 52 (bottom), 57, 65, 69, 80, 93 (bottom), 99 (top), 111 (bottom), 113, 119 (right), 129 (bottom), 130, 131 (top), 132 (bottom), 145, 150, 157, 158, 160 (bottom), 166, 167 (top), 173 (top), 174, 179, 181 (top), 182, 184 (top), 184 (bottom); Lyn and Exmoor Museum: 10 (top), 62, 105 (right), 117, 151, 155, 160 (top); Lynton and Barnstaple Railway Association: cover (back bottom), 143 (bottom), 146 (bottom); Lynton and Lynmouth Cliff Railway: 180; Lynton United Reformed Church: 102; Ken Newell: 77; Edward Nightingale: 49 (left), 67 (right), 76, 105 (left); North Devon Athenaeum: 12, 15, 21 (top), 21 (bottom), 25 (left), 30, 46, 47 (top), 48, 78 (right), 123 (top), 139, 140, 141 (bottom), 142 (top), 142 (bottom), 143 (top), 149, 161, 170 (top), 170 (left); Phyllida Ovenden: 70, 71, 72 (top), 73 (bottom), 74, 107; Hope Pedder: 95, 175 (top); Richard Pope: 124; Bill and Eileen Pryor: 93 (top), 106, 109, 132 (top), 146 (top), 168, 172 (right); Jenny Robinson: 29 (bottom); Valerie Robson: 51 (left), 63, 64 (left), 64 (right), 119 (left), 120 (top), 154, 162, 164 (left), 165; Mike Simpkins: 99 (bottom), 131 (bottom), 159, 163 (top), 167 (bottom); Ann Thorne: 28; Torquay Museum: 53, 54, 56, 89 (top); John Travis: 9 (bottom), 11, 14, 20 (top), 20 (bottom), 29 (top), 31, 35, 36, 39, 42, 47, 55, 67 (left), 68, 81, 84 (bottom), 89 (left), 90, 96 (left), 96 (right), 97, 110 (bottom), 116 (left), 125 (top), 153, 164 (right); Bruce Woolaway: cover (front top), 9 (top), 58, 126.

Introduction

'This town doesn't have a history!' Many times these words have been spoken. Yet nothing could be further from the truth. The past lives on in Lynton and Lynmouth. It shapes the character of the resort and still enriches life there today.

This is not a history of invading armies and double-dealing national politicians. It is the story of ordinary folk struggling to make a living in the hostile environment of the Exmoor coast.

Lynton and Lynmouth's history is one of change, of a small farming and fishing community being transformed into a select and fashionable resort. Yet it is also the story of continuity, for still today in Lynton and Lynmouth survive many traces of the distant past.

This is the history of the enterprising inhabitants who worked hard to build an attractive holiday resort in what had been a remote and almost inaccessible location. It is also the story of wealthy strangers, drawn by reports of spectacular scenery, who came for a short visit and stayed for many years.

Above all else it is the story of a community which was often torn apart by conflict. Clashes arose between locals and incomers, the lord of the manor and his tenants, priest and parishioners, developers and conservationists.

Out of these struggles was shaped the Lynton and Lynmouth we know today. It is a living and vibrant community which looks forward, and yet is steeped in history.

A Series of Disasters

IN THE eighteenth century the parish of Lynton was little-known and little-visited. Situated on a remote stretch of the North Devon coast, it was over fifty miles from the main tourist route, which ran through Exeter and Plymouth. A more isolated parish would have been difficult to find. Located in the heart of Exmoor, it was separated by almost twenty miles of barren moorland from the small towns of Ilfracombe to the west, Barnstaple to the south-west and Minehead to the east.

The parish was large. Some 11¼ miles in extent it stretched from the Bristol Channel up to the open moor. It was sparsely populated, having only 481 inhabitants in 1801. This was despite the fact that the parish included the small villages of Lynmouth and Lynton.

Lynmouth crouched beneath steep cliffs; a cluster of fishermen's cottages grouped around a small harbour. Here the moorland waters of the East and West Lyn met before rushing into Lynmouth Bay. A small herring-fishing fleet was based at this tidal inlet.

Lynton was perched at the top of a 450-feet-high cliff. There stood the parish church of St Mary the Virgin. Behind the church, sheltering in a hollow, was a farming community with thatched cottages grouped round three farms.

Just inland were the hamlets of Lynbridge and Barbrook, both sited on the banks of the West Lyn and both harnessing the fast-flowing waters to drive water mills. Beyond these hamlets lay a scattering of farms on the edge of the moor.

Wheeled vehicles were unknown in this remote district. Carts could not travel there, for there were no roads of any sort across the uplands. The twin villages tried to be self-sufficient but some essential goods were brought on the backs of packhorses, using ancient track-ways across the moor.

The sea was a much more important means of access and some bulky goods were landed from small sailing vessels. From South Wales came coal for heating. Also from the Welsh coast came limestone, which was heated in the kilns to produce the lime the farmers put on their acid soils. From Bristol came those foodstuffs, clothes and household goods which could not be produced locally.

The harbour was also the principal outlet for local products: wool from Exmoor sheep, bark from local oak trees to be used in the tanning industry, timber which went to South Wales for use as pit props in the coal mines, and barrels of cured herrings which went to Bristol for export.

In the second half of the eighteenth century a series of disasters struck this remote parish. It seemed almost as if fate was conspiring to destroy the local

Lynmouth in 1813. Small vessels brought supplies into the harbour. There appears to be a lime kiln on the east bank, but it is possible that red herrings were cured there.

economy. The spectre of ruin stalked through Lynton and Lynmouth. Some saw little hope for the future.

Torrential rain caused one disaster. The river at Lynmouth 'rose to such a degree as was never known by the memory of any man'. The raging waters of the Lyn swept down 'great rocks of several tons each' which completely choked the harbour. They plucked up boats and carried them away. Most serious of all, they eroded part of the stone jetty which sheltered vessels from westerly gales. As the flood waters rushed on and out to sea they left in their wake a small

Lynton in 1801. St Mary's Church overlooks the sea, but the farms and wool-spinners' cottages shelter in a hollow.

Lynmouth, c.1830. Goods brought in by sea were carried by packhorses up the hill to Lynton. Fishermen are drying a net on the jetty.

it is taken from a report of an event which took place in the early summer of 1770. History has a habit of repeating itself, but unfortunately man does not always learn from past experiences.

Lynmouth's tiny harbour was devastated and the implications were grave. Many men and boys earned their living as fishermen. Others were employed on the sailing vessels which traded between Lynmouth and other harbours on the Bristol Channel coast.

coastal community in a 'ruinous condition'.

This catalogue of destruction might well be an account of the flood disaster suffered by Lynmouth in August 1952. In fact

Small wonder then that in August 1770 the seamen of Lynmouth petitioned John Short, the lord of the manor, asking for help in repairing the jetty and pointing out that otherwise 'the seamen and other families must entirely leave'. John Short lived at Exeter and was reluctant to spend money on this remote fishing creek. He grudgingly agreed to hire masons to

Lynmouth in 1809. The two-arched bridge across the East Lyn was used by travellers who had followed the track-way down Countisbury Hill.

The New Inn on the bank of the East Lyn at Lynmouth, c.1820. This inn was in existence as early as 1778, which was before tourists began to arrive.

rebuild the foundations of the jetty, but only if the seamen would do all the labouring work without charge. He also instructed his local steward, William Litson, to ensure that the work was done as cheaply as possible.

The repairs to the jetty were completed by 1772 but cannot have been adequate, for by 1775 it had again been damaged by the waves. This time Mr Short absolutely refused to spend any more money on the harbour.

In desperation William Lock, a Lynmouth merchant, paid for a few essential repairs out of his own pocket so that his vessels could continue trading. The harbour, however, was still in a run-down condition and remained so until 1792 when William Lock took the decision to purchase the manor of Lynton from the Short family. Almost at once he put in hand a much more substantial reconstruction of the jetty.

As if the consequences of the 1770 flood were not enough to contend with, Lynmouth also had to cope with a dramatic decline in fish catches. For centuries it had depended on the enormous shoals of herrings which had appeared regularly in the Bristol Channel in the months of September and October. In 1630 Lynmouth had been described as being 'notable for the marvellous plenty of herrings there taken'. The herring fisheries

The yard at the rear of the New Inn, Lynmouth, c.1819. Early tourists found very primitive conditions in the twin villages.

were still flourishing in the early eighteenth century and employed many local people. Yet in 1753 it was reported: 'The herring fail, no fish caught'. Thereafter the herring shoals acted unpredictably, deserting the coast for years on end, only to return for a few summers in great numbers.

For as long as anyone could remember there had been a fish-processing industry at Lynmouth. Herrings caught in times of plenty had to be cured to preserve them. Lynmouth had specialised in 'red herrings'. These were produced by first salting the fish and then smoking them over smouldering oak fires. Small quantities of 'white herrings' had also been made, by pickling the fish in barrels of salt. Vessels had regularly taken cargoes of cured herrings to Bristol for export to the West Indies and the Catholic countries of southern Europe.

Early eighteenth-century manorial papers list a number of 'red houses' at Lynmouth. These were the buildings where the 'red herrings' were produced. The same records also mention some cellars, which were used for salting the herring and for their cool storage until they could be shipped away. A document of 1735 shows the leases for these 'red houses' and cellars being sold for substantial sums, indicating that at that time herring-processing was still a prosperous industry.

When the herring fisheries failed in the period after 1753, so too did the the fish processing industry. A rent-roll of 1774 indicates the extent of the collapse. It still lists no less than nine cellar properties, but only two were let, one was 'tumbled down', another was 'in ruins' and five more had no tenant. No 'red houses' are listed, only two buildings which were 'formerly red-herring houses'.

Large shoals reappeared in 1787 and in the next decade Lynmouth Bay was once again 'one mass of herrings'. Commercial herring processing resumed and boat loads of cured herring were once more sent to Bristol for export. The catches were so plentiful that the lord of the manor used the surplus to fertilise the field in front of his manor house. Superstitious locals were shocked at this behaviour. They blamed the disappearance of the herring shoals in 1797 on the 'insult offered to the fish by using them as manure'. This was an unlikely explanation, but the fact was that the herrings were never to return in such huge numbers again. The local economy had been dealt a serious blow.

The times of huge catches had gone for ever. There were still a few occasions when reasonably sized herring shoals ventured up the Bristol Channel. On Christmas Day 1811, for example, the church service was brought to an abrupt end on the congregation hearing that a shoal had entered the bay. However, such events became increasingly rare. Hardly ever were herring caught in large enough quantities to warrant an export trade. Usually there were barely sufficient to salt down for local needs. In the 1870s the last 'salting house' was cleared of two tons of salt and herring curing at Lynmouth finally came to an end.

There was also an oyster fishery at Lynmouth, but this was never big enough to provide much work. Some oysters were raked up in Lynmouth Bay and more were to be found off Porlock. In 1797 oysters were being sold in Lynmouth at two shillings per hundred and some were being shipped to other Bristol Channel ports. Yet by this time the natural stocks were already depleted. It was becoming apparent that in future the Lynmouth fishing industry would be unable to provide employment for more than a handful of men.

In exactly the same period the local woollen industry collapsed. Exmoor sheep had long provided the wool that the women spun on spinning wheels in their cottages. The yarn the spinners produced was supplied to the weavers of Barnstaple for manufacture into baize, serges, flannels and other cloths. William Litson was the local dealer. He bought wool from the farmers, supplied it to the spinners and then sold the yarn in Barnstaple.

Two factors caused the Lynton and Lynmouth spinning industry to fail in the last decade of the eighteenth century. Firstly, the Devon woollen industry faced growing competition from the new and highly mechanised Yorkshire mills. Secondly, in 1793 the outbreak of war with France cut off Continental markets. Barnstaple's cloth-production slumped and this meant that there was no longer a demand for yarn. So Lynton and Lynmouth's spinners were thrown out of work and the farmers could no longer sell the wool which had provided much of their income.

Times were hard. The local woollen industry had become a victim of economic and political upheavals at precisely the time that the herring fisheries were a casualty of natural change. The twin villages seemed cursed with misfortune and for a time the inhabitants could see no hope for the future.

The First Tourists

IT WAS at this time of economic crisis that the first tourists began to arrive. Never can strangers have been so welcome. How affluent they must have seemed to the poverty-stricken inhabitants of Lynton and Lynmouth! It was not long before a few shrewd locals realised that there was money to be made from these wealthy visitors.

Political upheavals on the Continent were partly responsible for tourists first seeking out Lynton and Lynmouth. It was the start of the French Revolution in 1789 which persuaded some members of the English gentry that instead of exploring Europe it might be safer to go on tours in their own country. Then in 1793 war broke out with France and for most of the next 22 years it was virtually impossible for the English to visit much of Europe. Those who had previously enjoyed travelling through Italy, the Alps and the Rhine Valley were now obliged to seek

This early description of the resort was published in Picturesque Views on the South Coast of England *(1826). It calls attention to the mild climate and scenic beauty.*

adventure in little-known regions of their own country.

A change in artistic fashion also helped to bring tourists to Lynton and Lynmouth. Some members of the leisured class were

Drawn by W.Collins R.A.   Engraved by W.B.Cooke.
Published March,1,1824, by J.& A.Arch, Cornhill.

LINMOUTH, OR LYNEMOUTH,

On the North coast of Devon, lies at about an equal distance from Ilfracombe and Minehead, being a little sea-port on the banks of the Lyn, where it falls into the Bristol Channel. Sheltered by abrupt hills and rocky cliffs, the scattered cottages which compose this singular and picturesque village, are blessed with a mild climate and a fruitful soil; peach trees adorn every wall, and snow is seldom seen there. The romantic village of Linton crowns the mountain which shelters this vale, and enjoys increasing reputation as a Watering-place, on account of its singular beauty and salubrity. Gainsborough (in a letter to Uvedale Price) pronounces it "the most delightful school for "a Landscape-painter this country can boast." Its "valley of stones," beautiful cascades, and magnificent rocks, well deserve this praise.

Lynmouth, c.1833. A few wealthy incomers have built large houses, but many local people still live in humble cottages.

becoming interested in seeking out scenery which would make attractive subjects for pictures, and might therefore be described as Picturesque. Desolate uplands such as the Lake District and Snowdonia were beginning to attract those looking for views to sketch, paint or simply to admire. Exmoor, having previously been avoided by travellers like Defoe as 'filthy barren land', was another remote area of the country which was now perceived as an attractive area to explore in search of the Picturesque.

John Swete, a wealthy South Devon clergyman, was a typical member of the new cult. He travelled to all parts of the county in his search for fine views to paint and describe in his journals, which he entitled *Picturesque Sketches of Devon*.

He was an early visitor to Lynton and Lynmouth, first arriving in 1789 and returning in 1796. Swete had discovered an artist's paradise. He wrote: 'Here every feature was romantic and picturesque … the landscape artist will dwell on them with unabating rapture'.

Swete's journals were only shown to a select circle of friends, but before long Lynton and Lynmouth's scenic attractions were being made known to a wider public. In 1797 William Maton was the first writer to praise the twin villages' spectacular landscapes in a travel book. Dr Maton was particularly impressed with the scenery of the 'Valley of Stones' and devoted nine pages to an account of this gigantic cleft running parallel to the Bristol Channel coast. His descriptions

Valley of Rocks, Lynton, c.1828. This valley was thought to be one of the wonders of the West of England. Notice the suggestion of a stone circle beneath Castle Rock.

were soon being plundered by other travel writers and this sudden acclaim persuaded some adventurous tourists to make the difficult journey to this remarkable dry valley.

Reports of stone circles in the Valley of Rocks also excited public curiosity. In 1789 John Swete had noticed 'several circles, large masses of stone, in diameter above forty feet … which seem to have been appropriated to the uses of the Druids'. Travel books soon began to suggest that this valley was a place where the Celts had practised their rites. These reports attracted many amateur antiquarians. Some fancied they could identify altars used in ancient sacrifices and gazed in wonder at what they considered to be stone circles erected by prehistoric man. Others felt a 'thrill of awful admiration' for what they saw as the

work of Nature. Opinions differed, but the resulting debate lured in new tourists to see for themselves these stone structures.

Romantic poets were also among the early visitors to Lynton and Lynmouth. Samuel Taylor Coleridge and William Wordsworth were staying in Somerset in November 1797. Wordsworth later recalled: 'Coleridge, my sister and myself started from Alfoxden with a view to visit Lynton and the Valley of Stones … in the course of this walk was planned the poem of the *Ancient Mariner*'. Captivated by Lynton and Lynmouth's pristine scenery they repeated the thirty-mile walk several times in the following year.

Robert Southey followed in their footsteps in 1799 and was equally impressed. He wrote: 'Lynmouth, a little village on the coast, is the most interesting place I have yet seen in this country'. He marvelled at the Valley of Rocks describing it as 'a spot which, as one of the greatest wonders of the west of England, would attract many more visitors if the roads were passable by carriages'.

In the summer of 1812 Percy Bysshe Shelley arrived at Lynmouth with Harriet, his child bride. Shelley wrote soon after his arrival: 'This place is beautiful … The climate is so mild that myrtles of an immense size twine up our cottage and roses blow in the open air in winter'. Shelley was inspired to pen *Queen Mab*.

Soon Shelley began to write a pamphlet advocating revolution. At a time when his country was at war with France such an act was illegal. He corked copies of his tract in bottles and launched them into the sea in the hope that they would be found and read. Worse was to follow. He sent his Irish servant, Daniel Hill, to Barnstaple to have his pamphlet printed so that it might be distributed to a wider readership. The authorities were alerted. Having seen a copy of the printed pamphlet, they had Daniel Hill arrested when he returned to Barnstaple. When Shelley heard the news he fled by sea to Wales. He left without paying the £200 fine which would have released his servant from Barnstaple Gaol.

Early visitors found it extremely difficult to find accommodation. When John Swete arrived at Lynton in 1789 he found that there was only one 'little public house at Lynton called the Crown where, though the accommodations are but indifferent, the people are civil and attentive'. He commented:

It cannot but be an object of request that a better inn and even lodging houses were built on the plain at Lynmouth for … if the roads for a few miles round were made more passable … I know no place more likely to be resorted to in the summer months.

William Litson, the Lynton wool dealer, was the first to meet the growing need for proper tourist accommodation. Faced with the collapse of his wool trade he decided to set up a new business. In 1800 he opened a small inn on the site where the Globe Inn now stands. He also furnished the adjoining cottages and let them to visitors. William Litson's new business prospered and in 1807 he built the Valley of Rocks Inn to meet the growing demand. In the following year he advertised his new inn in the *Exeter Flying Post*:

William Litson returns his grateful thanks to the nobility, gentry and public in general for the great support he has received the past seven years, and respectfully informs them for their better accommodation he has at consid-

Advertisement for the Valley of Rocks Hotel, c.1832.

The Valley of Rocks Hotel c.1840. This inn had been opened in 1807.

erable expense erected a large and convenient house in a desirable situation commanding most delightful sea and land prospects, which he has furnished with good beds and every other requisite and has lain in a stock of choice wines and liquors.

A tourist from Bath was among the visitors to this hotel in 1810. He arrived exhausted after losing his way crossing the 'dreary barren waste' between Barnstaple and Lynton. He recorded in his journal: 'Some good ale, a mutton chop, and Tenby oysters from the opposite coast of Wales soon made me forget the fatigues and labours of the day'. The success of William Litson's hotel and lodging-houses prompted other local people to provide accommodation for visitors. Lynton and

Lynmouth began to build a reputation as an infant resort catering for a small but discriminating clientele.

It was about this time that William Ashford Sanford made his first visit to Lynton. This wealthy member of the landed gentry was the owner of Nynehead Court in Somerset. He was a sick man and his doctors had recommended the fashionable remedy of taking the sea air. At Lynton Mr Sanford fell in love with the view. From John Lock, the lord of the manor, he acquired a cliff-top site commanding magnificent sea and river views. There he built a large house which he called Lynton Cottage.

William Sanford and his wife Mary were the first members of genteel society to build a house in the resort. They were

Looking up the West Lyn valley at Lynmouth, c.1838.

in residence every summer and played host to the rich and famous. In so doing they gave the infant resort a stamp of approval which soon encouraged other fashionables to have houses built there. A Mr Fotte built a cottage beneath the Lyn Cliff and sold it in 1817 to Robert Herries who lived there for many years, greatly improving both the house and grounds (now known as Glen Lyn). In 1826 the Rev. W.S. Halliday visited Lynton and, being charmed by the scenery, built a house on the cliffs which he called Clooneavin, an Irish word meaning 'happy rest'.

Lynton and Lynmouth began to grow. Between 1801 and 1841 the population of the parish increased from 481 to 1,027. 'Many houses of tolerable appearance have within a few years been built for the accommodation of guests; there are also several respectable inns,' reported one traveller in 1830.

Up at Lynton the old farming village had been set back from the cliffs. The cottages had nestled in a depression where they were sheltered from gales. Yet the wealthy incomers were more interested in fine views than with seeking protection from the elements, so the new hotels, lodging-houses and villas were erected on sites looking out over the Bristol Channel.

Down at Lynmouth building plots were

Lynmouth, c.1838. On the far right is Prospect House.

scarce, for the cliffs rose steeply from the sea and river. In 1828 work began to construct a new road along the harbour and river. This opened up some new sites for development. In the next decade attractive lodging-houses were erected all the way along the river.

Signs of the old economy were still in evidence. Visitors to Lynton occasionally encountered herds of cattle being driven in to be milked at the farms in the old village. At Lynmouth a few fishermen

Left: The first Lyndale Hotel in the mid-1830s. It stood near the harbour and in later years was known as Beach House.

Below: Lynton, c.1840. Older houses cluster in the hollow, but newer ones for the visitors have been sited where they command sea views. The castellated building on the left is a lodging – house called Summit Castle. Lower down the hill is the vicarage.

Lynmouth from the bridge over the East Lyn, c.1840. It is becoming a genteel resort.

Lynmouth in the mid-1870s. The Lyndale Hotel is on the left.

could be seen pottering about in boats. Yet it was clear that the twin villages were steadily changing as tourism became the most important activity.

Not everyone welcomed the change. While the development of a new resort created job opportunities, some thought that the changes were not for the better. It was suggested that the appealing innocence of country folk living close to nature was being corrupted by grasping greed. Visitors complained when they found themselves being accosted by locals touting for trade. In 1851 one guidebook found it necessary to caution the approaching visitor:

> At Lynton telescopes are employed at the rival houses for the prompt discovery of the approaching traveller. He had better therefore determine beforehand on his inn, or he will become a bone of contention to a triad of postboys, who wait with

LYNTON.—On Monday last, the extensive and commodious premises, newly-erected by Mrs. Jones, the proprietor of the Valley of Rocks Hotel, called "the New Lyndale Hotel," were opened for business. The accommodation at this attractive watering-place is greatly improved, and among the principal in this respect must be ranked "the New Lyndale," situated at the bottom of the hill leading from Lynmouth to Lynton; or rather close by Lynmouth Bridge, commanding very extensive, choice, and varied scenery of the sea, and the splendid wild scenery for which Lynton is so famed. Mrs. Jones, the well-known proprietor of the Valley of Rocks, also conducts the business at the new establishment which will be found by visitors to be second to none in the North of Devon, and we wish Mrs. Jones success in her new undertaking.

News item from the Exeter Flying Post *in June 1854 announcing the opening of the new Lyndale Hotel. It had been built on the site of the New Inn.*

additional horses at the bottom of the hill to drag the coach to its destination.

The clock could not be turned back. For better or worse, a small but exclusive resort was emerging which was catering for a select clientele, who alone could afford the time and cost of the difficult journey.

Early Road Travel

FEW resorts were as hard to reach by land as Lynton and Lynmouth. At the end of the eighteenth century the journey there was an adventure that only the most intrepid tourists set out on.

The whole of North Devon was virtually cut off from the outside world. The roads were deeply rutted, pitted with craters and strewn with rocks. In 1801 Charles Dibdin, a travel writer, commented: 'The roads are so dreadful that the difficulty of getting there is scarcely repaid by a view of so charming a county and thus the inhabitants seem as if they were in voluntary exile'.

Barnstaple was the gateway town for the North Devon coast, but not until 1778 was there a coach service to this town from Exeter. In 1787 it took the coach over twelve hours to cover the 39 miles separating the two centres.

Further problems lay ahead for those who wanted to travel on to Lynton and Lynmouth. As late as 1805 these coastal villages were still some ten miles from the nearest roads, so tourists had to travel there on foot or on horseback. Horse-drawn carriages had never been seen there.

Some of the early visitors to Lynton and Lynmouth described the atrocious condition of the ancient track-ways they followed across the moor. In 1796 John Swete noted in his journal that the approach to Lynmouth 'resembled more the bed of a torrent than a travelled way'. In 1801 John Skinner arrived on a visit from Somerset and commented: 'To travellers not accustomed to a mountainous country the approach to this place would have been deemed impassable'.

When William Sanford made his initial visit to Lynton and Lynmouth he was the first to try and travel there in a wheeled vehicle. With great difficulty his carriage was taken across the moor to Countisbury and even down the steep descent to Lynmouth. There he found that due to the lack of a proper road it was quite impossible for the carriage to go any further. The horses had to be taken out of the shafts and a gang of men carried it up the cliff-side track to Lynton.

In the period after 1815 local people decided that carriage roads had to be built to make it possible for more tourists to reach the resort. No turnpike trust was prepared to invest money in constructing highways to such a remote area so Mr Lock, the lord of the manor, began the work. It was, however, Mr Sanford and a few more public-spirited residents who built, widened and improved most of the new roads.

One of the most important improvements was the building of a road between

The top of Lynmouth Hill, c.1832. The roads shown here had been made about 1820. The construction of new roads in the 1820s and 1830s at last made it possible to reach the resort in a horse-drawn carriage.

Lynton and Lynmouth. The principal link between the two villages had been the track which started at the harbour, climbed Mars Hill and then zigzagged up the cliff to the church, but about 1820 a new road was made up Lynmouth Hill. At the top of the hill the road split, with one branch going into Lynton while the other went to Barbrook and on in the direction of Barnstaple. So this road also provided a new way out of the two villages, taking the place of the old route along Lydiate Lane and then over the commons to Dean.

The new road along the river, c.1832. Work began to construct this road in 1828. Large lodging-houses were soon built on fine sites that had been made more easily accessible by the road.

The ratepayers of Lynton and Lynmouth also played their part. At a vestry meeting in 1828 they decided to construct a new road from the harbour along the river to connect with the new road up Lynmouth Hill. Some of the old cellars where herring had been salted were destroyed in its construction.

Another major improvement was the construction of a carriage road along the side of the East Lyn Valley to Watersmeet and Hillsford Bridge. This road was made in 1837 and was paid for by the Revd John James Scott, a wealthy assistant curate at Lynton. It seems likely that he had it built to enable carriages to reach his fine residence at Combe Park. John Knight then had this road extended over the

Advertisements from two rival hotels in the North
Devon Journal *of 19 August 1833. Lynton hotels
sometimes sent out men to greet tourists in the hope
of obtaining patronage. The men had horses with
them to help pull the visitors' carriages up the hills.*

*The Valley of Rocks Hotel in the early 1860s. Many
guests arrived in private carriages.*

moor to Simonsbath to improve the access to his Exmoor estate.

As soon as roads began to be built, a few carriages began to make their way along the new roads to the resort, though at first only with great difficulty. In 1823 Mrs Selwyn, having travelled the breadth of Britain, complained: 'The drive from Ilfracombe to Lynton is through the worst of roads. It exceeded all we had met with … the horses being fatigued, the drivers gave them beer, two large jugs divided among the four'.

Every few miles wealthy visitors like Mrs Selwyn would have to hire new horses to pull their private carriages. These rented horses were known as post-horses and were obtained at roadside inns known as post-houses. All the hotels in Lynton and Lynmouth had large stables where they kept post-horses.

Public-transport services also were gradually introduced. By 1830 the track-way over the moor to Barnstaple had been improved sufficiently for a public 'conveyance' to be able to run there three times a week.

It was the opening of the Bristol and

Roads serving the North Devon resorts in 1835. Lynton and Lynmouth was still many miles from the nearest turnpike.

Ilfracombe, 1881. Visitors still had to complete their journey to Lynton and Lynmouth by coach. Sam Colwill, the driver in the top hat, for many years operated the service to Lynton. His son Tom is the driver of the second coach.

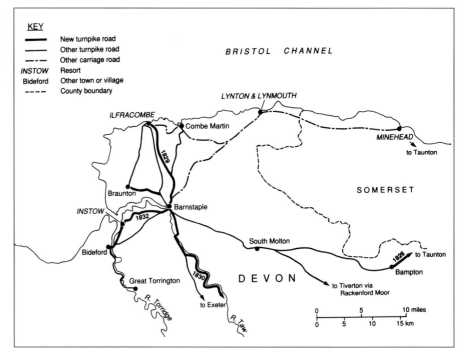

Coaches about to leave Tom Jones's coach office, c.1910.

Exeter Railway as far as Taunton in July 1843 which prompted the start of Lynton and Lynmouth's first proper coach service. A light coach began running to the new station at Taunton to meet trains from London and Bristol.

On 12 July 1854 the North Devon Railway from Exeter to Barnstaple opened. Almost at once a connecting coach service began operating between Lynton and Barnstaple station. Lyntonians looked forward to an 'overflowing summer' with one newspaper correspondent writing that 'the only drawback to the influx of strangers

hitherto has been the difficulty of access'. Unfortunately the new line failed to give the hoped-for boost to the resort's tourist trade. The route via Exeter and Barnstaple was a long, circuitous one and Lynton was still at a serious disadvantage compared with South Devon resorts like Torquay and Teignmouth, which by this time were connected to the main rail network.

Some of the early Lynton coachmen made a point of having a drink whenever the coach stopped for a change of horses. A local curate wrote an amusing account of a trip on a coach operating in the 1850s between Lynton and the railway station at

Coach climbing Lynmouth Hill in 1911.

To the Directors of the Lynton and Barnstaple Railway Co.

GENTLEMEN,

We, the Committee appointed by the inhabitants of Lynton, at a public meeting held in the Foresters' Hall, Lynton, on 15th July, 1894, to collect Statistics of Traffic to and from Lynton during the previous year, beg to report that we have collected the same with great care, with the following result :—

Passengers by Barnstaple Coaches (Jones)	...	...	...	7,000
„	Ilfracombe	„	(Copp)	...	10,380
„	„	„	(Colwill)	...	5,868
„	Minehead	„	(Baker)	...	3,605
„	„	„	(Heywood)	...	1,570
„	Dulverton	„	„	...	800
„	Posting Carriages	...	...	...	4,018
„	„	from Minehead, Dunster, South Molton, and Porlock			850
„	Cabs and Hackney Carriages	...	...		692
„	Landed by Steamers	...	...	...	7,000
					41,783

Goods landed by Vessels at Lynmouth ... .. 4,200 tons.
„ by Road from Barnstaple (Jones) ... ... 176 „
Mails and Parcel Post amount to 6cwt. per day.
The Cliff Railway carried over 100,000 passengers between Lynton and Lynmouth.

N.B.—All the above traffic has since been greatly increased.

Yours obediently,

(Signed) JOHN HEYWOOD,

Statistics collected in 1894 to help assess the need for a railway. They show the relative importance of coach services from different towns. Note that substantial numbers were also arriving by private carriage or by steamer.

Bridgwater. The coach was driven by a man called Warwell:

We left Lynton at about six a.m., and Warwell had beer at Countisbury, beer again at Porlock, Minehead, Dunster, Williton, Putsham and Cannington. What he consumed in the couple of hours during which the coach waited at Bridgwater I do not know, but on the return journey he had hot spirits at every place where in the forenoon he had called for beer. We reached Lynton about ten p.m., and he congratulated himself to me on his self-restraint in the matter of drink. He never took spirits until he turned

LYNTON, LYNMOUTH, AND BARNSTAPLE.

THE WELL-APPOINTED FAST FOUR-HORSE COACH,

"TANTIVY,"

carrying the mails, runs daily throughout the year (Sundays excepted), in connection with the trains of London and South-Western Railway.

THE ONLY DAILY ROUTE THROUGHOUT THE YEAR FROM AND TO LYNTON AND LYNMOUTH.

The "GLEN LYN" and the "TALLY HO!"

Additional Coaches run during the SUMMER SEASON ONLY.

MESSRS. JONES BROS.' FAST FOUR-HORSE COACHES ...		A.M.	P.M.	P.M.	The Coaches meet Trains at Barnstaple Junction.	To LYNTON.		
	"TANTIVY," (all the year round) dep.	8 0	...	...			A.M.	A.M.	A.M.
	"GLEN LYN," ⎰ during the sum- ⎰ „	...	1 45	...	WATERLOO LONDON dep.	...	9 5	11 0
	"TALLY HO!" ⎱ mer season only ⎱ „	...	...	5 0	Portsmouth .... „	...	8 0	10 40
	Barnstaple Junc. arr.	11 0	3 0	8 0	Southampton .... „	...	8 25	11 33
FROM LYNTON	TRAINS—				Salisbury .... „	...	11 20	1 5
	Barnstaple Junction ......dep.	11 13	3 21	8 17	Exeter (Queen St.)... „	6 50	1 45	3 20
Via LONDON AND SOUTH WESTERN RAILWAY.	Okehampton............arr.	2 44	5 12	10 22	Plymouth (North Rd.) „	...	11 42	...
	Launceston (*via* Halwill) „	4 0	9 32	...	Tavistock .... „	...	12 31	...
COACHES leave the Company's Booking Offices, Churchill, Lynton, every Week-day.	Tavistock .... „	3 15	5 49	10 48	Launceston(*via* Halwill „	...	10 15	...
	Plymouth (North Rd.) „	3 42	6 30	11 16	Okehampton .... „	...	1 9	...
	Exeter (Queen St.)........ „	12 39	4 54	9 57	Barnstaple Junction arr.	8 23	3 21	4 33
THROUGH BOOKING.— Passengers can book to Lynton from stations on this system.	Salisbury .... „	2 49	8 3	...	COACH.— Barnstaple Junc. dep	8 25	3 35	5 0
	Southampton .... „	5 26	10 12	...	LYNTON Lynton arr.	11 0	6 30	7 40
	Portsmouth .... „	6 30	10 56	...				
	WATERLOO LONDON arrive	5 0	10 15	...				

A coach timetable, c.1892.

This photograph of 1906 shows a coach picking up passengers at the Lyndale Hotel before setting off up Countisbury Hill.

backwards as some people did; but he could never abide their drinking ways, so he said.

Lynton and Lynmouth's continuing isolation was emphasised in 1874 when the resort's nearest rivals both gained railways, Ilfracombe being linked to Barnstaple, and Minehead to Taunton. Ilfracombe and Minehead both enjoyed a sudden influx of visitors, but Lynton and Lynmouth could no longer compete on near equal terms and had a poor season.

By this time Lynton and Lynmouth was further from the nearest railway than almost any other resort in England. It remained a small, select watering-place, attracting discriminating visitors who preferred to holiday out of reach of the railway at quiet resorts far-removed from working-class day-trippers.

Coach services multiplied in the continuing absence of a railway. Services started running from all the leading hotels. From the Valley of Rocks Hotel, for example, coaches ran to Barnstaple and Ilfracombe, while from the Royal Castle Hotel coaches went to Minehead. After the railway line from Tiverton to Dulverton opened in 1884, coaches began running from the Lyndale Hotel to connect with the trains at Dulverton.

By the 1890s Lynton and Lynmouth was claiming to have more coach services than any other town in England. In most

A coach about to set off for Minehead from the Royal Castle Hotel in the Edwardian era.

parts of the country coaches had long been replaced by trains but here they were still in use. For many visitors the ride over the moors was the highlight of their holiday.

Yet the days of the coach were numbered. Soon it would be threatened by the belated arrival of the train. Not many years would pass before the first motor vehicles would begin to struggle up the hilly roads leading to Lynton and Lynmouth.

Sea Travel

THE Bristol Channel provided an alternative way of reaching Lynton and Lynmouth. A few early visitors found it quicker and cheaper to travel there by sea rather than attempt the difficult land journey. They came in private yachts or on one of the small trading vessels which linked Lynton and Lynmouth with Bristol and South Wales. Others travelled on a sailing packet from Bristol or Swansea to Ilfracombe and then completed their journey by land. Sail,

though, was dependent on the vagaries of the wind, and in the early days never more than a trickle of visitors reached the resort by sea.

It was the advent of steamship services on the Bristol Channel which made Lynton and Lynmouth much more easily accessible. In 1822 the *Duke of Lancaster*, a steam packet, started calling at Ilfracombe on her passages between Bristol and Cork. By 1830 Lynmouth had a service. The paddle-steamer *Glamorgan*

A view of the bay from the Castle Hotel, c.1840. Steamers had been calling at Lynmouth for at least ten years.

Steamship timetable for 1852. Departures from Bristol and Ilfracombe were at a different time each day. This was because steamers could only reach Bristol at high tide. Steamers only called at Lynmouth when weather permitted.

began calling on its passage between Bristol and Ilfracombe. In the next decade packet steamers *en route* from Bristol to both Bideford and Cornwall also began to call at Lynmouth.

Competition between the rival steamship companies reduced fares and thus made it possible for more visitors to reach the resort. For many years the fare between Bristol and Lynmouth was 10s. best cabin and 5s. fore-cabin, which was about a third of the cost of the journey by coach.

Facilities for disembarkation at Lynmouth were very poor. Steamers had to anchor out in the bay, while passengers were brought ashore in small craft. This meant that Lynmouth was a port of call for fewer packet steamers than Ilfracombe, which had a proper harbour.

Yet, despite the landing difficulties, a substantial proportion of Lynton and Lynmouth's visitors preferred to travel there by sea rather than face the long, slow journey by land. This is why the numbers of visitors from Bristol and nearby Bath steadily increased. There was, however, a problem with these early steamer services. They only operated for a short summer season. The resort tended to empty out when the last steamer left at the end of September.

Sea travel to Lynton and Lynmouth was significantly improved by developments further up the Bristol Channel. In 1867 a railway was constructed from Bristol to Portishead. A pier was built at Portishead in the following year and a low-water extension was added by the spring of 1870. These improvements meant that, instead of steamers departing from Bristol and having to leave at high water to navigate the Avon, they could sail from Portishead at any state of the tide. This enabled departures to be at a fixed time each day.

The service from Portishead began in August 1869. By July 1870 the Cardiff and Portishead Steamship Company was advertising that the steamer *Ely* would leave Portishead at 1.30 p.m., after the arrival of trains from Bristol, the Midlands and London, and would call at Lynmouth

The harbour at Lynmouth in the Edwardian era. A steamer can be seen out in the bay.

on its way to Ilfracombe. The fares were remarkably cheap: only 3s. single and 4s. 6d. return for the best cabin. This proved to be an extremely popular way of travelling to Lynton and Lynmouth, lessening the journey time from many parts of the country.

In 1885 the Great Western Railway took over the Portishead steamers, after buying up the Bristol and Portishead Railway, and at the end of the 1886 season announced that it was terminating its steamer service to North Devon. This was a devastating blow. In the absence of a railway, Lynton and Lynmouth had relied on this steamer service to bring in a substantial proportion of its visitors. The 1887 season was a disaster, with hoteliers and lodging-house keepers complaining that many of their regular visitors from Bristol, Bath, the Midlands and London had deserted them.

Yet sea travel to North Devon did not come to an end with the passing of the Portishead steamers, for their place was taken by a growing number of pleasure steamers. Although a few long-stay visitors took advantage of these excursion steamers, most of the arrivals on these vessels were trippers who were present for only a few hours.

Day trips by steamer to Lynmouth were not a recent innovation. As early as 1849 the wooden tug *Haswell* had ferried a party of seventy day-trippers from Swansea. In the early days nearly all the excursionists were from South Wales, as Lynmouth was too far down the Channel to be reached by a day-excursion from Bristol.

It was, however, the introduction of fast, purpose-built pleasure steamers in the period after 1880 which transformed the excursion trade. Some of these

Lynmouth harbour, c.1919. At high tide boats could leave from the harbour when ferrying passengers out to the steamer.

commodious vessels operated from South Wales ports, often in conjunction with local railway companies. Others began running from Bristol, for these powerful steamers could reach Lynmouth in less than four hours, which at last made a day trip a practical proposition.

As the number of excursion steamers increased, so local businessmen began to agitate for a pier, in the hope that improved landing facilities would encourage more of these vessels to call at their resort. They knew that some of the steamer companies disliked taking trippers to Lynmouth, where the operation of landing them in small boats was a slow procedure even in calm weather and impossible if it was rough. It was obvious that most steamers preferred to call at Ilfracombe, where large numbers of passengers could easily be landed at the harbour, particularly after a new deep-water pier was built there in 1873.

The tradespeople of Lynton and Lynmouth hoped that a pier would open their resort to a wider cross-section of society. Some even claimed to prefer the 'hard-working clerk and mechanic to the half-starved aristocrats that get a half-pension from the government and who come here and put on airs'.

Most of the resident gentry and wealthy visitors, on the other hand, regarded all day-trippers as a threat to the social tone of the resort and strongly opposed the calls for a pier. They viewed with horror the drunken trippers sometimes landed from what were locally-known as 'floating beershops'. Their fear was that a pier would result in far larger numbers of working-class excursionists being disgorged from the steamers to disrupt the quiet gentility of the place. This elite group made it clear that they wanted Lynton and Lynmouth to remain the 'monopoly of the select few who come to rusticate for a month or two'.

Despite the fact that Parliamentary sanction was obtained for five different pier schemes, Lynmouth never acquired good landing facilities. In part this was because of doubts about the financial viability of a pier, but it was mainly because of strong opposition from wealthy residents, who wanted to preserve the exclusive character of the resort. Their success in keeping out day-trippers was to be clearly shown on Whit Monday 1901, when only 50 people came ashore from

Passengers being ferried out to a steamer, c.1906. At low tide it was necessary to scramble over the rocks to reach the boats.

the steamers at Lynmouth, as compared with 800 landed at the new pier at Minehead and 2,000 invading Ilfracombe.

Smuggling

ON THE remote Exmoor coast smuggling was rife in the early nineteenth century. It was almost impossible to keep watch over the many small coves, and the lack of good roads meant that it was difficult for Customs officials to move quickly when they suspected the smugglers were about to run contraband in. Lynmouth was practically cut off from the outside world and the inhabitants thought that what went on there was no one else's business.

Laws passed by a far-away Government imposing heavy duties on imported luxuries, such as brandy, rum and tobacco, were deeply resented. Few saw anything wrong in making handsome profits by avoiding these taxes. Some enjoyed the excitement, danger and camaraderie of belonging to a smuggling gang. Some welcomed the presents of silk,

Lynmouth, c.1828. This remote harbour was sometimes used by smugglers.

fine handkerchiefs and brandy they received for hiding men or contraband when the need arose. Others simply turned a blind eye, out of loyalty to their fellow locals and a deep suspicion for Government officials.

Armed vessels owned by Irish smuggling syndicates had the biggest share in the Bristol Channel smuggling. From France they brought brandy and wine. From Ireland they brought tobacco, tea, salt and soap.

Then there were a number of fishing vessels from Cornwall and the Channel Islands which crossed to Brittany and returned with a cargo of contraband. The rewards were high, for these vessels could make more money running a single illicit cargo into a remote North Devon cove than they could earn by fishing for a month.

On occasions armed French vessels from Roscoff and Brest were known to venture as far up the Bristol Channel as Lynmouth with a cargo of contraband. Yet for them the danger was much greater, and more often they would take their cargo to the notorious smugglers' base on Lundy for transshipment onto an English vessel.

Ilfracombe pilot cutters were also actively involved in local smuggling. They had to meet ships entering the Bristol Channel to put pilots on board to guide the ships up to Bristol. This provided ideal opportunities for the pilot cutters to pick up goods on which no duty had been paid, which they then distributed all along the North Devon coast. Many barrels of rum were unloaded off vessels returning from the West Indies, and many boxes of tobacco were unloaded off ships returning from Maryland and Virginia.

Some of the coastal traders that plied between the Bristol Channel ports also carried smuggled goods hidden under their normal cargo. Some would visit Lundy to pick up contraband. Others would rendezvous with a smuggling vessel far out at sea and then bring in the contraband.

Sometimes fishing boats pottered along the coast pretending to pull in their lobster pots, when really they were hauling up a string of brandy kegs that had been submerged and marked by a float. It was quite impossible for the preventive men to keep check on all the small vessels operating in inshore waters.

Accounts of local smuggling are hard to find. The nature of the clandestine work meant that only on the rare occasions when smugglers were caught red-handed were their activities reported in the newspapers. Yet there is sufficient evidence to indicate that smuggling was supplementing the income of many local people.

The records show that in the eighteenth century the chief Customs officer at Ilfracombe frequently reported to his superiors that smuggling was going on at Lynmouth. With the limited resources at his disposal he was powerless to stop it.

Not until 1805 was a riding officer stationed at Lynmouth. His job was to patrol the local coast on horseback looking for smugglers. Soon he was reporting that he had found casks of brandy hidden at the bottom of the cliffs and in hedgerows. Here was proof of smuggling. Yet catching men in the act of smuggling was very difficult in an isolated area where the close-knit local community seemed to give them active support.

In 1809 the Customs Service at last had an important success. The excise cutter

Lynton and Lynmouth in the early 1840s. Night and day these cliffs were patrolled by coastguards on the look-out for smugglers.

Resolution from Milford Haven was patrolling the North Devon coast when a suspicious lugger was sighted. It gave chase but lost the sailing vessel in a sea mist. Many hours later the lugger was found beached at Lynmouth. It was the *Mary Ann* of Fowey and it had just completed landing some 600 barrels of brandy. William Lilburn, the Commander of the *Resolution*, had to decide whether to seize the lugger or to land his men and take possession of the brandy. He decided that the vessel was the principal prize, put some of his men on board and then escorted it into Ilfracombe. By the time the Custom's men returned to Lynmouth the brandy had disappeared and not a cask was subsequently found. In his report to the Excise Board in London, Commander Lilburn accused the Lynmouth riding officer of seriously neglecting his duties and suggested he was actually in the pay of the smugglers.

Soon after this a preventive boat was stationed at Lynmouth. In 1813, while patrolling off Glenthorne, it discovered six kegs of illicit brandy which had been submerged to await collection by a local boat.

Glenthorne was always a favourite landing place for the smugglers. This wild and lonely cove was virtually inaccessible by land and had a large recess into the cliff which the locals called 'Smugglers

Glenthorne, c.1832. The Revd W.S.Halliday built this house in 1830 after receiving a large inheritance. Smugglers ran many cargoes in on this lonely stretch of coast.

Cave'. On many a dark night smugglers would lie watching on Foreland Point, waiting for an incoming schooner. Hour after hour they would strain their eyes peering out into the darkness. A triangle of three lights high on a ship's mast was the sign they looked for. As soon as they saw the glimmering signal out at sea, they would light three lanterns rigged to a triangular frame on a donkey's back. Backwards and forwards the donkey would be walked, until once again they saw the triangle of lights shining back across the waves. Then they would set off along the cliffs, using the lanterns on the donkey to lead the vessel towards Glenthorne.

Once the contraband was ashore the smugglers would lash it to their packhorses and set off along little-known moorland track-ways into inland Devon. Only very rarely were these 'gentlemen of the night' caught. In 1818 there was a report of a John Whittle being arrested while moving contraband goods in the parish of Brendon. He was fined £10 for smuggling. What was more, he received six months hard labour for assaulting the Excise Officer who had tried to arrest him.

The lonely coves to the west of Lynmouth were also used to bring in contraband. At the end of November 1827 a large cargo was run in at Heddon's Mouth, probably by a French vessel.

Thomas Martin, the Lynmouth riding officer, heard about this run and began to make enquiries. A few days later, accompanied by several members of the Ilfracombe coastguard station, he raided John Hoyles' farm at Trentishoe. After a lengthy search they found the entrance to a cave in a stable. In the underground chamber were hidden 38 tubs of brandy. John Hoyles was arrested, but he asked for permission to change his clothes before being taken to gaol. He went into a back room of the farmhouse and escaped through a window.

The following day the painstaking search continued. When the coastguards moved piles of unthreshed corn in a barn they discovered the entrance to another cave. In it they found 174 tubs of brandy and gin. Two days later in a cowshed they found a hiding place containing 50 tubs of spirits and four casks of wine.

That afternoon the coastguards set off for Ilfracombe with the first seven cart loads of the seized tubs. They deposited the contraband at the Custom House. Late that evening they were about to return to Trentishoe for a second load when they were attacked with stones and staves by a 300-strong mob. John Hoyles was a member of the hostile crowd. He was never captured. Some said that he fled the country.

It was in 1832 that the coastguards had their best chance to capture large numbers of smugglers red-handed at Lynmouth. Watching from the cliffs at Ilfracombe they spotted a vessel sailing up the Bristol Channel. For some reason their suspicions were aroused. They rode along the coast, following it until it anchored off Lynmouth. There they had someone hail her and he was told that the vessel had a cargo of china clay and was bound for Gloucester. They were not convinced and lay in hiding.

Part way through the night the three coastguards saw a number of farmers with packhorses assemble on Lynmouth beach. Then they saw a boat come to shore loaded with over thirty kegs of brandy. The coastguards rushed out and managed to seize the kegs and also three packhorses, though in the darkness the smugglers escaped. Help was urgently needed. So while two of the customs-men guarded the contraband, the other mounted one of the packhorses and rode off to Porlock to seek reinforcements.

Soon after this another boat came ashore and that too started to unload kegs of brandy. When the crew realised that there were two coastguards on the beach, they attacked them and severely beat them. At this point the farmers returned, reclaimed their two packhorses, loaded them up with 64 kegs of brandy and disappeared into the night. The crew returned to their vessel, leaving the injured coastguards lying on the beach.

The vessel immediately set sail and made off along the coast, putting in at Appledore where she landed the remainder of her cargo before sailing out to sea. The Customs and Excise subsequently recovered the forty kegs landed there.

The *Exeter Flying Post* carried a report of this smuggling run. It stated that the vessel was a large pleasure yacht and was believed to be 'the property of a gentleman of Appledore'. Yet there is no subsequent reference to any Appledore gentleman being convicted of smuggling. Perhaps he had influence with the local magistrates and was able to escape prosecution.

Records do show that shortly afterwards

Packhorses like these were used to carry contraband from the coast to moorland farms and inland villages.

Michael Sullivan, the Lynmouth riding officer, seized three horses carrying 64 kegs on Countisbury Common. Two farm labourers were leading the horses. They claimed not to know how the goods had been landed or who owned the horses. They said that they had simply been paid to pick up the kegs at a certain spot and leave it at 'the cross-roads on the road to Brendon'. But it was clear that this was the contraband which had just been landed on Lynmouth beach. The two farm labourers were obviously small pawns in an organization dominated by powerful local men. Yet it was these two labourers who had been caught and it was they who appeared in court. They were convicted of smuggling but their fines were immediately paid. Could it have been the mysterious Appledore gentleman who found the money and so bought their silence?

By the 1850s smuggling had been virtually stamped out. Over thirty coastguards watched the coast between Bude and Porlock. The Lynmouth detachment alone consisted of a chief officer and five boatmen. The likelihood of being caught had greatly increased. At the same time the rewards were decreasing, for the Government had adopted a free-trade policy and was steadily reducing the duties on many imported goods. Smuggling died out because it was no longer worth taking such grave risks. Yet, although only the memories survived, the romance lived on. Many old Lynmouth seafarers fascinated Victorian visitors with tales of successful smuggling runs.

The Revel

IN THE early nineteenth century the Lynton Revel was the highlight of the year. Merrymakers came from far and near, for this was an opportunity to forget the hardships of everyday life. The festivities began on the first Sunday after Midsummer Day and could last for up to a week.

Practically everyone attended church on Revel Sunday. All eyes turned to watch the entrance of the wrestling champion from the previous year. He had the honour of wearing the winner's hat, to which were attached the six silver spoons to be wrestled for that afternoon.

A barrel of ale was waiting near the church gate after the service. It was soon drained. Then the crowd munched revel cakes, made with dark flour, currants and caraway seeds, before moving down to the Globe Inn. Outside the tavern some played skittles, and some tried their skill on the shooting range, while others bought gingerbreads and comfits from stallholders. The majority milled around talking excitedly, maybe listening to blind William Bale from Kentisbury playing his violin and waiting for the start of the wrestling match.

Soon the two wrestlers would be heard approaching. Usually they were both local men. Nathaniel Vellacott, a farmer from West Lyn, often carried off the prize in the 1830s.

The crowd would part to let the competitors through. Ringmasters made the people form a circle and kept them back with large sticks, cracking the shoulders of those who encroached on the ring. Now the wrestlers could be seen. They were burly, muscular men stripped to the waist. On their heads they wore red and black caps.

The Devon wrestling the crowd watched was not for the faint-hearted. Kicking was the main form of attack. Shoes were worn and usually these had been soaked in bullock's blood and baked to make them as hard as possible. Often they were tipped with iron. Legs were bandaged or even wrapped in carpet to give some protection. This was a competition calling for brute strength, agility and a complete disregard for pain.

The object was for the wrestler to kick hard and often, until his opponent's shins were left pouring blood and he was so weakened that it was easy to throw him to the ground. Three times he had to be thrown, 'three fair backs' being the term used to denote victory.

The winner was given the silver spoons to wear. He also received a purse with a few gold sovereigns. To a country man accustomed to earning some nine shillings a week these prizes represented a small fortune. They had to, for these wrestlers would not risk their limbs for a few coppers.

In the 1840s the Lynton Revel came under fierce attack from Victorian reformers, just as similar festivals did at many other Devon villages. It was the heavy drinking and physical violence that was most objected to. By 1849 the *North Devon Journal* was denouncing the revel

Queen Street in the early 1860s. The sign of the Globe Inn can be seen. The building on this side of the inn was a farm. Note that many of the buildings are thatched.

as an 'offensive and demoralising remnant of barbarous times'.

Once the rich residents withdrew their financial support, the Lynton Revel was doomed. In 1853 Thomas Cooper, a Lynton doctor, wrote that until recently large prizes had been raised by subscription, but 'of late the prizes have not been beyond a few shillings collected from the people on the ground. This of itself has given a death-blow to the Revel'.

Conflict

NO ONE could have foreseen the troubles that were in store when in 1792 the Lock family of Lynmouth acquired the manor of Lynton from the Short family. Ahead lay a series of damaging disputes which were to bedevil the history of the twin villages for the next hundred years.

At first the inhabitants rejoiced that the manor had come into the hands of a local family. No longer would they have to rely on a steward to relay their problems to the Short family in distant Exeter.

Yet all too soon the locals had good reason to complain. The Lock family greatly increased the rentals for all the houses and farms owned by the manor.

Worse was to follow. In 1799 William Lock assigned his manorial rights to his son John Lock, who immediately announced that he intended to enclose part of the commons. The inhabitants were furious when they heard the news.

The Valley of Rocks, 1829. This was part of the Lynton commons so local farmers had the right to graze animals here.

From time immemorial the local farmers had rights to graze their animals on the commons. These ancient communal rights were now under threat.

By July 1800 John Lock had coerced the majority of his tenant farmers into signing, or putting their mark, to an agreement to enclose the Lynton commons. Each farmer was to receive a part of the 'waste' in proportion to the acreage of land he farmed. The agreement stated that the enclosure of land was optional. Yet the document made it clear that those who chose to enclose the parcel of land allotted to them would lose their rights to turn out cattle on the remainder of the commons, and would retain only the right to 'turbary', that is the right to cut peat for fuel.

The ink was hardly dry before John Lock was making plans to enclose some of the land allotted to him. The land designated as his included part of the Valley of Rocks and his first step was to put an ugly stone wall round an area there known as 'The Warren'. He claimed that he needed to do so in order that he might have a private supply of rabbits. Feelings ran high at what was seen as an act of vandalism. Tourists came to admire the wild grandeur of the valley and now it had been desecrated.

Visitors were quick to complain at the damage done to this beauty spot. In 1802 an artist declared: 'On entering the Valley of Stones the eye is offended by a quadrangular wall … not a single blade of

The Valley of Rocks, c.1852. John Lock had erected the walls at the beginning of the century. Many felt that the wild beauty of the valley had been desecrated.

grass rises on it, to break its natural deformity and relieve the eye from so disgusting an object'. Some claimed that 'immense Druidical stones and circles' had been removed to be used in the building of these walls, or to be sold for use as gate posts.

Not content with this, John Lock went on to enclose a total of 90 of the 150 acres allotted to him. He had made sure that he had been awarded the common land that was near to Lynton. He realised that, with tourists coming in increasing numbers, fat profits could be made from enclosing and selling prime sites overlooking the sea for development.

In one deal alone John Lock recouped most of the money his father had given for the whole manor. In or about the year 1815 William Sanford paid John Lock £200 to obtain a lease on a plot of land

with a superb view, on which he was to build his summer residence known as Lynton Cottage. Then in 1826 Mr Sanford paid a further £980 to acquire the freehold on this site and other surrounding land measuring twelve acres in total. So John Lock had received from Mr Sanford a total of £1,180. In 1792 the Lock family had paid only £1,300 for the whole manor.

What annoyed the tenant farmers even more was that the lord of the manor flouted the agreement he had put his pen to. Despite the fact that he had enclosed more than half of the land allotted to him, he still continued to graze just as many animals on the rest of the common. Most of the other farmers had decided not to enclose, probably because they thought that the cost of putting up walls would be more than the value of their land when

The Lynton Cottage, c.1830. Mr W.A.Sanford had this house built here after visiting Lynton and being impressed by the spectacular views.

Lee Abbey, c.1853. Charles Bailey had this imposing country house erected in the early 1840s. The octagonal music room was added about 1851.

enclosed. They were angry that once John Lock had finished making enclosures he conveniently forgot the existence of the agreement.

In 1853 a bitter dispute broke out over the remaining commons. It was Charles Bailey who stirred things up. He was a land agent who had made his money advising the Sanfords and other landed gentry how to run their estates. In 1841 he had decided to become a country gentleman himself and had purchased a

The Valley of Rocks, 1860. Visitors liked to walk and ride here, so any threat to enclose the valley was treated very seriously.

farm known as Ley Barton and another at Six Acre from Dr John Clarke, a local landowner. He had built a fine country house and had given it the somewhat pretentious name of Lee Abbey.

Charles Bailey was now entitled to graze animals on the Lynton commons, but he was concerned that his sheep might become infected there by running with the numerous 'scabbed' sheep belonging to other farmers. He therefore decided to try and obtain general agreement for an enclosure of the remaining common land. Many of the farmers now seemed to favour the idea, but the manor house firmly opposed it.

As a land agent Charles Bailey had an excellent understanding of enclosure procedures. He decided that the best way forward was to petition the Enclosure Commissioners seeking their sanction for a division of the commons. In January 1854 an Assistant Commissioner held public meetings at the Valley of Rocks Hotel to hear objections to the proposed enclosure.

There were many who wished to object. The hoteliers and lodging-house keepers expressed their fears that Charles Bailey planned to wall off the western part of the Valley of Rocks, thus preventing tourists from visiting it. Opposition also came from those representing the owners of the manor. By this time John Lock had died and his sister Mary was the lady of the manor. She was married to the Revd Thomas Roe, Rector of Brendon, and this elderly cleric feared that most of the remaining manorial powers would be lost, if the remaining common land was enclosed.

Then Mr Bailey gave his arguments for enclosure. He denied wanting to enclose part of the Valley of Rocks and explained why he believed it would be better to divide up the remainder of the common land. His lawyer produced evidence showing that, after the agreement of 1800, the lords of the manor had enclosed much of their share of the commons.

After hearing all the arguments the Assistant Commissioner went away to consider the case. In March of that year came the news that the Commissioners had held the agreement of 1800 to be a valid one, and that, if the majority of those with rights on the commons so wished, then the remainder of the waste could be enclosed.

The Roes did not give up easily. Although elderly and in ill-health, they decided to take the unusual step of actually taking the Enclosure Commissioners to court. The case was heard in March 1855. The Roe family won because it was held that, as owners of the manor, they had a right to object to any enclosure of the commons.

The Revd and Mrs Roe did not live to benefit from their victory. Thomas Roe died in January 1855, even before the case was heard, and his wife died in September. Whether the pressure of the

The Valley of Rocks Hotel in 1859. Several meetings about the proposed enclosure of the Valley of Rocks were held here in the 1850s.

The road to Watersmeet, c.1840. It had been built in 1837.

case hastened their end it is impossible to tell.

The manor then passed to Mrs Roe's son, John Colwell Roe, who decided that he would be happy to allow the remaining commons to be enclosed, if he received a good share of the land. In September 1856 a meeting of the Enclosure Commissioners was held at the Valley of Rocks Hotel to assess all claims. All parties agreed that the remainder of the Valley of Rocks should be left unenclosed so that the public could enjoy it for all time. After lengthy negotiations, agreement on the division of the remainder of the commons was also reached.

By 1860 work on enclosing the commons was well under way. Gangs of navvies were brought in to erect stone walls across the heather and gorse moors. The local police put one of these labourers in the stocks near the church when he refused to pay a fine for being drunk. There Isaac Stacey remained all day, probably the last person to be confined there for an actual offence.

New problems arose once the enclosure had been completed. Robert Roe had succeeded to the manor in 1858 on the death of his brother, and he seemed determined to gain every advantage possible from his position as lord of the manor. The road to Watersmeet ran over land allotted to him in the enclosures and so he claimed that he owned the road, even though neither he nor his predecessors had ever contributed a penny towards its construction or upkeep. In 1861 he erected a gate at the start of the road and chained it. Then he put up a table of tolls and appointed a collector to demand the money from all who used the road.

The toll gate was a serious threat to the local economy. Horses and coaches had to pay dearly for the privilege of taking visitors up the valley to Watersmeet. Packhorses were charged each time they struggled up the valley with a load of lime or coal for some moorland destination. Even the poor working man returning to Brendon after a hard day's toil had to pay to walk along the road.

This time the whole community united in opposition to the lord of the manor. On 23 October 1861 the people of Lynton and Lynmouth took the law into their own hands. A crowd gathered and marched to the offending barrier. The *North Devon Journal* reported that the 'gate was speedily cut down and the toll box removed' and that this 'caused great joy among the inhabitants who celebrated the triumph by a bonfire in the evening'.

Three days later the people assembled to decide on their next step. General Rawdon, an elderly gentleman living at Clooneavin, was elected to the chair. He was a former M.P. and a man of considerable influence, so there were loud cheers when he declared that the lord of the manor had no right to stop up a right of way. The applause was even greater when General Rawdon announced that he would fight to 'assist the weak when they are right against the strong when

Watersmeet, c.1850. The house was erected about 1832 by the Revd W.S.Halliday. It was used as a hunting and fishing lodge.

they are wrong'. This time the inhabitants had powerful support. The lord of the manor had to back down and allow people to travel freely along the road. He had suffered a major defeat.

Harbour Disputes

THE harbour was to trigger off even more serious disputes between the lords of the manor and the local inhabitants.

As early as 1817 John Lock had begun to demand a keelage fee from all vessels using the harbour and a toll on all goods imported or exported through Lynmouth. A painted table of tolls was set up on the new tower on the stone jetty in the early 1830s. The lord of the manor's water bailiff was given the title of harbour master and was expected to collect the dues.

The lords of the manor justified these charges by claiming they had to spend large sums maintaining the jetty, which protected the harbour from the sea. They also pointed out that, whenever necessary, they renewed the posts marking the deep channel running into the harbour. Most important of all, they claimed that being lords of the manor they had a legal right to charge tolls.

This attempt to charge harbour dues was deeply resented by the Lynmouth traders, who felt that the lords of the manor were trying to gain an unfair business advantage. The lords of the manor had shares in several Lynmouth vessels and largely owned the principal coal-merchant business, for which they imported the coal. They had a monopoly in the import of limestone and owned the lime kilns at Lynmouth. They were also heavily involved in other import and export businesses. The traders feared that the harbour dues were intended to raise the price of their goods and thus enable the lord of the manor to undersell them.

The tenants of the lord of the manor were obliged to meet their landlord's demands for harbour dues, or risk losing

The Rhenish Tower in the late 1880s. Notice the board which in the past had been used to display a list of harbour tolls.

The lime kilns at Lynmouth in the early 1860s. They were still in use at this time. The timber in the foreground may well have come from local oak woods. Pit props were exported to South Wales for use in coal mines.

their tenancies, but many other fishermen and traders tried to find ways of avoiding payment or simply refused to pay.

Thomas Geen was one of the leaders of the fight against the tolls. Born and bred in Lynmouth, he had worked as a young man for John Colwell Roe, a son of the lord of the manor. In the early 1840s he had left Mr Roe's employ and set up on his own account as a builder and sea-trader. One dark night in 1843 Mr Roe caught Geen unloading a cargo of slates and flooring stones which was being imported for the National School then being built at Lynton. Mr Roe was furious, for he had had a monopoly in the import of building materials. 'I'll soon put a stop to that!' he declared. A few days later Geen received a bill for importing forty tons of slate at 8d. a ton. He reluctantly paid the bill, but vowed never to pay a toll ever again.

Another view of the lime kilns, c.1870. Much more lime could be transported by horse and cart than had been possible by packhorse.

Time after time the Roes billed Thomas Geen for harbour dues, and time after time he refused to pay. Finally, in 1855 they begun legal proceedings against him.

This stretch of beach was sometimes used for landing cargoes. This photograph is c.1885 and shows the sea front before the first part of the esplanade was built.

Vessels alongside the jetty, c.1865.

Shortly before the case was due to be heard, Geen decamped from Lynmouth and was not seen again for many months. The Roe's solicitor advised them to drop the case, pointing out that Geen was 'not worth a shilling' and they could not expect any money from him if they won the case. So the Roes were left with a heavy bill for legal expenses and seething with anger that Geen had outsmarted them.

When Robert Roe inherited the manor of Lynton in 1858, he at once made it clear that he intended to profit from his position. He had been away for many years, serving as a sea captain, but after returning he was soon involved in disputes which for a time threatened to destroy the maritime trade and also the tourist industry.

It was a quarrel between Captain Roe and his neighbour, the Revd Walter Halliday of Glenthorne, which triggered off the trouble. They fell out over the question of who was entitled to wreckage washed up at Lynmouth. The problem arose because the manor house and grounds of the lord of the manor of Lynton were not situated in the manor of Lynton. They were on the east side of the Lyn, on land within the the manor of Countisbury. The Revd Halliday was lord of the manor of Countisbury and he disputed Robert Roe's right to wreckage found on the shore of the manor grounds at Lynmouth. With neither party prepared to give way, the Board of Trade was asked to settle the dispute. In the summer of 1863 an official inquiry was held at the Valley of Rocks Hotel. Locals were agog at the spectacle of the two leading landowners at loggerheads. After an extremely costly nine-day hearing, Robert Roe won the case. The two gentlemen were left with a mutual dislike.

The Revd Halliday soon hit back. He sent his bailiff to Robert Roe to demand a sixpenny rent he claimed to be owed for Robert Roe's grounds, as they were in the manor of Countisbury. A trifling sum, but he was trying to score a point. His unfortunate bailiff received a frosty reception at Robert Roe's manor house!

Robert Roe was demanding dues from all harbour users. Soon he began to suspect that the Revd Halliday was seeking to get even by encouraging Geen and other locals to refuse to pay harbour dues at Lynmouth.

The feud continued. In 1866 the Revd Halliday employed Thomas Geen to construct lime kilns on the beach at Glenthorne, and also a road from there across the moor to Brendon. Three years later Geen completed the construction of a breakwater to provide a small harbour by the lime kilns. This expensive project was obviously intended to take much of the local lime trade away from Robert Roe's lime kilns at Lynmouth.

In August 1869 matters finally came to a head when Thomas Geen took Robert Roe to court. Nominally this was an

The harbour in the early 1870s. Notice the shingle and boulders that had been swept through a breach in the jetty. It was no longer possible for vessels to berth alongside the jetty.

action against Roe for the illegal seizure of Geen's timber, but in reality it was intended to test at law the right of Robert Roe to levy dues at Lynmouth Harbour. At the outset Robert Roe's lawyer made it clear that his client believed that it was Walter Halliday who was putting up the money to enable Geen to fight the case.

The incident which led to the case had arisen when Thomas Geen's vessel had come into Lynmouth harbour with a load of sawn timber. As soon as work had begun to unload the timber, Robert Roe's men had appeared and had demanded dues. When Geen's men had refused to pay, some of the timber had been seized by Roe's men to pay for harbour dues.

The hearing at the Exeter Assizes lasted two days. Robert Roe's lawyer produced evidence to show that tolls had been paid since 1817. Thomas Geen's lawyer countered this by pointing out that nearly all those who paid harbour dues were tenants of the lord of the manor and had no option but to pay. He produced as witnesses a number of vessel owners and traders who stated that they had refused to pay.

Then Geen's lawyer sprang a major surprise. He produced in court a researcher, who had searched at the Public Record Office for documents relating to the manor of Lynton and had found no reference to either the Crown or

Parliament granting the right to charge dues. His evidence proved decisive and there was a verdict in favour of Thomas Geen.

Robert Roe was furious. He decided that if he was not allowed to charge dues then he would cease to maintain the harbour. That winter a severe storm breached a hole in the jetty and over 2,000 tons of shingle were washed into the harbour. This made it quite impossible for vessels to lie alongside the jetty while loading or unloading. In the past the lord of the manor had always kept the quay in repair. This time nothing was done.

Robert Roe was determined to get even with Thomas Geen. His first step was to send some of his men down to the beach to upset one of Geen's carts which was taking away a load of sand. He warned him not to take any more building materials from the shore.

Then Captain Roe turned his attention to another of Thomas Geen's businesses. He knew that Geen was an agent for the Bristol Steam Navigation Company and that each summer he ferried passengers between the steamers and shore. He also knew that when the tide was too far out for the landing boats to enter the harbour with their passengers, they were grounded in a channel specially made for the purpose. So when he saw a group of Geen's workmen clearing stones out of this channel, he instructed his manager, William Bevan, to take a gang of men and to completely fill it up with stones to prevent its use. This meant that passengers could not be safely brought ashore when the tide was more than half way out. It was an action that threatened everyone with a commercial interest in the holiday-makers arriving by sea, so not surprisingly feelings ran high in the resort.

I, the undersigned, **hereby give public notice** that no person do in future lade or unlade any goods on the Mole or Quay or on any part of the lands within the

MANOR OF LYNTON,

without the special license or permission of the **Lord** or his **Steward**, nor make fast any boat, ship, or vessel, to the posts, rings, or mooring places in the **harbour** of **LYNMOUTH**, nor take sand, stones, ore weed, ballast, or other thing whatsoever from the foreshore of the said **Manor** between high and low water mark without the like license and permission. **And I hereby further give notice** that all persons who shall in defiance of this Notice do any of the acts aforesaid without such license and permission first had and obtained, will be deemed **WILFUL TRESPASSERS,** and will be proceeded against according to law.

ROBERT ROE,

Lord of the Manor of Lynton.

Dated the 11th day of June, A.D. 1870.

TUCKER, Printer, Bookbinder, Bookseller, Stationer, &c., South Molton.

A poster published by Captain Roe forbidding anyone to use the harbour without permission. The taking of oreweed, for fertiliser; or sand, for building; or boulders, for ballast; was also forbidden.

In June 1870 Captain Roe went back to court to see if he could have the verdict overturned. This time the case was heard before the Court of Queen's Bench in London. Once again the court decided that the ancient documents indicated that the lord of the manor had no legal right to harbour dues.

Robert Roe's anger knew no bounds. He published posters declaring that, as he was not allowed to charge tolls, then no vessels were to unload goods at the harbour without his express permission.

There was almost open warfare at the

The Nautilus, *c.1880. This vessel was partly owned by the lords of the manor. For many years it had brought cargoes into Lynmouth.*

harbour. Twice the *John* of Combe Martin arrived at Lynmouth with a load of coal for Thomas Geen. On both occasions Captain Roe ordered it not to enter the harbour but still it came in and discharged its cargo at the quay. Captain Roe claimed that Geen had a 'gang of roughs' present to guard the cargo while it was being unloaded.

Captain Roe then resolved to make it quite impossible for anyone else to use the harbour. In December 1870 a party of men under his personal direction rooted up all the mooring posts in the harbour. Then they set to work removing the posts which marked the entrance channel and were also used for warping vessels in and out. So the harbour was effectively closed to all vessels other than those of the lord of the manor. When his own vessels were sighted, branches were temporarily used to mark the channel and anchors were put down in the harbour with buoys attached for mooring purposes. On one occasion the *John* did risk trying to run a cargo in for Geen but it ran aground. So Geen and other local merchants were obliged to land their cargoes at other ports along the coast and then move them to Lynton by land, adding substantially to their cost.

The beach at Lynmouth, c.1880. The nearest boatman is standing by a pair of wheels which were probably used to help transport boats down to the sea. Notice the bathing machines.

Thomas Geen complained bitterly to the Board of Trade that he was being driven out of business. A Divisional Officer was sent from Ilfracombe to inspect. He reported: 'Mr Geen is backed up with money …by the Revd Walter Halliday of Glenthorne, a bitter opponent of Mr Roe …between the two the harbour is going to utter ruin'.

Eventually Board of Trade pressure forced Captain Roe to back down and allow free access to the harbour. He still did only the minimum necessary to comply. He replaced the posts he had removed at the entrance to the harbour but, instead of the stout oak posts which had previously stood there, he put in

'mere fir poles' which served to mark the channel but were utterly useless for warping in on. He still refused to spend his own money repairing the breach in the jetty, but when the inhabitants raised a subscription of £70 he allowed them to repair it themselves.

Captain Roe was not easily beaten and at this point he had a brainwave. Having had the courts twice declare that he had no legal right to levy tolls, he hit on a way of obtaining that right. In December 1871 he applied to Parliament for powers to build a 240-yard long landing pier running out into the sea from a point some 600 yards to the north-west of the harbour. This iron-piles pier would be sheltered from westerly gales by a breakwater. At first the inhabitants were delighted. Landing passengers and freight had always been difficult at Lynmouth for there was a 33-feet tidal range and at times a heavy ground swell. They felt that a pier would open the resort up to far more visitors and make it easier to import goods.

Only when they read the small print did they realise what lay behind the proposal. Captain Roe was applying to Parliament for legal powers to charge tolls on all cargoes shipped in or out of Lynmouth Bay, even if they were not landed or embarked by his pier.

Furthermore he proposed a very high toll of 1s. 6d. a ton on steamers as compared with 6d. a ton at Ilfracombe. Steamer companies soon made it clear that they would probably stop calling if this was to be the charge. There would also be heavy landing dues for all passengers. So his scheme was a serious threat to the local tourist industry.

The Provisional Order Robert Roe was seeking would also have given him the right to enclose and reclaim a large section of the foreshore to the west of the harbour, providing him with some valuable building sites right next to the sea. While he would have profited selling off plots for development, the resort would have suffered, for the coastal scenery which attracted the visitors would have been marred and the ladies' bathing beach to the west of the harbour would have been lost. What is more people would have had to pay to go on what was left of the beach.

A stormy protest meeting was held at which the inhabitants welcomed the idea of a pier but voiced their strong opposition to the rest of the proposals. A

A vessel being unloaded in 1883.

petition to the Board of Trade was organised and not surprisingly Thomas Geen and Walter Halliday were among the first to sign. The strong local opposition caused the Board of Trade in March 1872 to send a civil engineer to Lynmouth to conduct an inquiry.

Following this inquiry the Board of Trade deliberated on whether to grant Captain Roe his application. Fortunately for Lynton and Lynmouth, the officials at the Board saw through his scheme. They recommended that Captain Roe be given permission to construct both the landing pier and a breakwater, but declared that his proposal that he should be allowed to tax all shipping and goods landed anywhere in the bay was 'absurd' and recommended that he should only be allowed to charge tolls at the pier, and that the harbour and the rest of the beach should be free from all tolls. They also advised that the public should continue to be allowed free access to the beach and that most of the tolls for vessels, freight and passengers should be reduced from the excessive rates proposed by Captain Roe.

At the beginning of May 1872, the Secretary to the Board of Trade gave notice that he would be bringing a Bill before the House of Commons containing these watered-down proposals. Before it could be heard Captain Roe died. He passed away after a sudden illness 'resulting from a severe cold and inflammation of the lungs'. He was only fifty-three.

Like both his parents, Robert Roe had died while in dispute with the local people. Whether the stress of the legal battles brought about his premature death it is impossible to tell. Parliament sanctioned the amended pier scheme but his widow never went ahead with it. She decided that, without the right to charge dues anywhere in the bay, the Act was not worth the paper it was printed on.

By a strange irony, only a few years later, those who had opposed Robert Roe's pier scheme in 1877 applied to Parliament for powers to build their own pier at Lynmouth. Thomas Geen and Walter Halliday were among the backers of the scheme, but it also had the support of most of the tradespeople. A Parliamentary Order was obtained giving official sanction to the scheme. Yet this proposal likewise came to nothing, partly because of opposition from some of the wealthy residents and partly because financiers refused to back it, because they felt that the revenue from the pier would never be enough to warrant the high capital investment.

Personalities

THE history of Lynton and Lynmouth is the story of its people. Yet it would need an extremely large book to do justice to the lives of every inhabitant. This chapter sets out to fulfil a much more modest task. It picks out just four leading personalities. By describing incidents in their colourful lives, it hopes to recapture the flavour of life in earlier times.

MATTHEW MUNDY (1797-1864)

Matthew Mundy came from a long line of South Devon clergymen. For many years it had been customary for the sons of the well-off Mundy family to enter the church. Matthew Mundy kept up the tradition. After graduating at Oxford, he was briefly the incumbent in two Devon parishes before being appointed Perpetual Curate of Lynton in November 1832. He was to serve the parish well for 28 years.

Matthew Mundy was a High-Churchman. One of his curates considered him kind but 'somewhat run to seed', and described him as 'a scholar, a moderate man in all things, a very good man of business, and fond of society'. His parishioners respected him. He was their adviser and friend.

A man of medium height and fair complexion, he was a hardy individual. Wet or fine, every day from April to December, he took an early morning dip at Wringcliff Bay. Careless of wind and rain, he thought nothing of making long journeys across the moor to take a service in a remote church. Usually he went on foot, but sometimes he would go on horseback.

There is an amusing tale about one such trip. Matthew Mundy had been asked to take a couple of services at South Molton Church. He set off on his cob, taking a short cut across the high moor. After preaching he left South Molton in the late evening and set off for home. Crossing Exmoor the Revd Mundy lost his way in a fog. Near Mole's Chamber he fell off his horse and broke his collar-bone. Unable to remount he was forced to walk. Mile after mile he tramped through heather and peat bogs. Towards midnight he saw a light in a cottage window. He banged on the door. A woman in a nightgown and nightcap opened the window.

'Who is there?' she called.

'It's Mr Mundy,' he shouted.

'Monday,' said she. 'Get away you drunken dog! It's still Sunday!'

She slammed the window and went back to bed leaving him to wander on. Not until breakfast did he reach Lynton. Mrs Mundy at once sent for a post-chaise and 'rattled him off' to Exeter, fifty miles away, where a surgeon set his collar-bone.

The Revd Mundy had not been long in Lynton before he decided that he needed a new house. The old parsonage was a dilapidated cottage, quite unfit for a

St Mary's Church in Matthew Mundy's time. This print is c.1839. The first north aisle had been added in 1817 and the second one in c.1833. The growth of the resort had made these extensions necessary.

The tumble-down old parsonage at Lynton, at the time the National School was built near it in 1844.

gentleman. It was let out to two labourers, and he and his wife were living in lodgings. He applied to the church authorities for funds to build a new one. In 1835 the new parsonage (now Garson House) was built on the perpetual curate's glebe at a cost of £1,150.

In 1841 Matthew Mundy was faced with a crisis. Ever since the National School was founded in 1818, the Hon. Mrs Knight, wife of John Knight, the owner of the Exmoor estate, had always met almost all of the expenses of the Lynton National School but, after her death in that year, the Knight family withdrew its financial support. This was a church school and Matthew Mundy was determined that it should not close. He asked the wealthy inhabitants to subscribe. Collections were

This sampler was made at the first National School. Needlework was an important part of the curriculum for girls.

made for the school whenever there were visitors in church. Still there was a shortfall and this he generously made up himself.

Two years later Matthew Mundy was given notice that the National School must vacate the house, between the Castle Hotel and the Church, that it had been using. Once again he refused to close the school. Instead he decided that the time had come to build an entirely new school building, on glebe land near the Crown Hotel. Grants were obtained, but the Revd Mundy also dipped into his own pocket to help meet the cost.

The new National School was opened in 1844. It must have been desperately cramped. The single classroom was intended to accommodate 144 pupils. In 1846 the school had 185 children on roll. Imagine trying to pack so many into one room!

At the annual inspection in 1847, 150 National School pupils were examined. The school inspector found that the Bible played a big part in the teaching. There were 49 pupils who could read 'Holy Scriptures with ease', but only 27 could read easy stories and only seven could read non-fiction. Yet the school was well above the average standard of its day. The inspector reported: 'This is a good school. The mistress was educated in the school, gives her whole heart to the work, and by the kind co-operation of the rector, is most successful'.

Matthew Mundy's main claim to fame was that he collected much of the information which was later to be used by R.D. Blackmore in his great romance, *Lorna Doone*. Soon after arriving in Lynton, the Revd Mundy realized that some of the oldest inhabitants had some remarkable tales to tell. He decided to write them down. William Cowell, a Lynton doctor, assisted him. Soon they realized that most of the stories had originated from an old woman called Ursula Johnson. She was reputed to be a witch and had died in 1826 at the age of 87.

People tend to dismiss the story of the Doones as fiction. Yet if some of it was fact, then Ursula Johnson would have known, for she had been born in 1738. That was less than forty years after the Doones were supposed to have left the area, and she would have talked to people who remembered them.

Matthew Mundy divided the tales into three groups, entitling them 'The Legend of De Wichehalse', 'The Legend of the Doones of Badgworthy', and 'The Legend of Faggus and his Strawberry Horse'. He had copies made by the senior girls at the National School.

Parts of these stories were published in Dr Cooper's Lynton guidebook as early as 1853, which was well before R.D. Blackmore wrote his romance. Blackmore probably saw a copy of the original manuscript when he holidayed in Lynton in 1865, for every incident recorded by Matthew Mundy was woven into

Blackmore's masterpiece, which was published in 1869.

Lorna Doone was to become a major success. In the late-Victorian era it would make Exmoor a fashionable holiday destination and would bring welcome business to the resort's hotels. The book was particularly popular with Americans and many toured the area seeking out the places described in its pages. By 1901 so many Americans were staying in the hotels that one newspaper commented: 'For five months in the year the Devonshire accent is now little more conspicuous than the American one'. So, in collecting the Doone stories, Matthew Mundy had unwittingly helped to put Lynton and Lynmouth on the map.

In 1860 Matthew Mundy left Lynton to become vicar of Rockbeare near Exeter. Sadly the transfer was not a happy one. He yearned for the rocky Exmoor coast and he was to die only four years later.

Lynmouth in the early 1860s. The house in the centre is Island Cottage where a few years earlier William Thornton had lived.

WILLIAM HENRY THORNTON (1830-1916)

William Thornton came from 'good stock'. Many members of his well-connected family had made their mark in the service of their country. Educated at Rugby and Trinity College, Cambridge, he graduated in 1853. Later that year, just when he was wondering what to do with his life, he had a letter from Mr Halliday of Glenthorne, an old family friend. It advised him that the Revd Mundy wanted a curate and the position was his if he wanted it.

In those days it was easy for a man of means to become a clergyman. William wrote to Matthew Mundy and it was soon agreed that he should take entire charge of the parish of Countisbury and from

time to time assist at Lynton, all for the less-than-princely stipend of £20 a year. Money, though, was not a problem, for William's father at once offered to give him a generous allowance of £200 a year. All that remained was for William to go through the formalities of sitting a 'voluntary theological examination' at Cambridge, and then to travel down to Exeter to be examined and ordained by the Bishop of Exeter. So there he was, a young man of 23, 'absolutely ignorant' of religion and life, as he himself admitted, and yet in sole charge of a parish.

After staying for a few days with Matthew Mundy, William arranged to rent Island Cottage at Lynmouth. For only £40 a year the proprietor, Mrs Bevan, provided the fully-furnished house, complete with coal for heating and with her own excellent cuisine thrown in. So William had the surplus income to live

Another view of Lynmouth in the early 1860s. On the right is Nelson's Cottage, so called because Earl Nelson, a descendant of Horatio Nelson, stayed there in 1841.

Mars Hill and the quay in the 1860s.

like a country squire. He rode on his favourite bay mare, shot game birds, climbed the cliffs looking for gulls' eggs, fished for trout and salmon, walked on the moors and went sailing.

Above all else William liked to socialise and, being both the local clergyman and a member of a 'good family', he had the entry into the homes of all the leading members of the local society. In this exclusive clique were old Mrs Sanford, of Lynton Cottage; General Rawdon and his wife, Lady Cremorne, who lived at Clooneavin; old Thomas Roe and his wife, who were in residence at the Manor House; Miss Angel Heath, a Latin scholar, who lived at Heath House; and the Revd and Mrs Mundy.

The local gentry sought William's company. He frequently visited the Hallidays at Glenthorne. Frederic Knight,

the owner of Exmoor, was a special friend and William would ride with him searching Exmoor in the vain hope that they would find rich reserves of iron ore.

Summer visitors also cultivated his friendship. He was often to be found sailing with Mr Snowden, a regular visitor from Bath. Sometimes he would hunt the red deer with Captain West, also of Bath, who each year arrived by sea with his pack of stag-hounds. Those were days when many Devon clergy rode after the hounds and locals saw nothing unusual in their curate taking part in traditional country sports.

Yet, despite all these distractions, William Thornton still found time for his duties. This inexperienced young man ministered to the sick and dying, preached to country folk in Countisbury Church, and sometimes to congregations of fashionable

Island Cottage in the late 1890s.

severe. One bitter evening, while travelling near Parracombe, he came across the Barnstaple mail coach which had overturned, leaving two horses half strangled by their harness and hanging over a ravine. He had to free and rescue the horses, find and attend to the driver who was lying unconscious on the road, and stand guard over the mail bags until help could be summoned.

His life was packed with incidents, but none was stranger than the occasion of the visit to Lynmouth by a Russian princess. This princess had decided to take a sea-water bath at the bath-house run by Mrs Trix near the harbour. After the princess had had her hot bath, Mrs Trix demanded ten shillings. This the princess refused to pay, pointing out that the price advertised in the window was two shillings and sixpence. Not at all overawed by royalty, Mrs Trix stood her ground and insisted on payment. With deadlock reached the curate was sent for.

William, for once in his life, felt nervous. He found the small but fiery Mrs Trix standing in the road with her hands on her hips waiting to do battle. She still refused to reduce her charge, pointing out that she had had to provide extra hot water and countless hot towels. Then a spokesman for the princess made the mistake of claiming that the bath had been dirty. 'Dirty!' screamed the indignant Mrs Trix. 'If it was dirty when she went in,

visitors in Lynton Church. The clergy for miles around were quick to take advantage of the eager young curate, who never charged a penny and was prepared to ride many miles in all weathers to take services.

William also took a keen interest in educating local children. Appalled by the poor standard of teaching in the little school at Countisbury, he decided to change things. The school was run by a Mrs Elworthy, the widow of a Lynmouth butcher, and the young curate decided that she knew 'positively nothing'. He asked Henrietta Hollier, a young Lynmouth spinster, to help him. Each morning they would toil up Countisbury Hill and spend several hours trying to turn unlettered country children into scholars.

William Thornton loved adventure and frequently found it. One wild night in the Arctic winter of 1854, he walked miles through snowdrifts to Glenthorne to give help to the crew of a barque which had been wrecked near the smugglers' cave.

The following winter was even more

William Thornton, c.1899.

Lynmouth for Simonsbath. The rich and poor alike had lost a friend. His charm, kindness and sense of fun would be much missed.

THOMAS BAKER (1803-1890)

Thomas Baker was a local man who successfully made the transition from farmer and shipowner to hotelier. Born in 1803 and reared in the parish, he began work at an early age. Day after day he would walk with his father, a farmer and

The Castle Hotel as it was in Thomas Baker's early years there.

what do you imagine was its condition by the time she came out?' This was too much for the young curate. He fled the field. The unfortunate princess had to acknowledge defeat and pay her bill.

The young clergyman had many good qualities, but he was headstrong and did not take kindly to criticism. So in February 1855 he was furious when Matthew Mundy took him to task for spending time collecting money for local boatmen who had rescued the crew of a doomed vessel. There and then he decided to start looking for a new post. It was not long before Frederic Knight was offering him the chance to become the first vicar of the parish of Exmoor. A new church was built at Simonsbath and early in the following year William Thornton left

carrier, as they led lines of packhorses carrying lime and coal. Perhaps the hard streak in his nature was developed then, for it was often bleak and cold tramping from the harbour up to the moorland farms.

By 1830 Thomas Baker and his father were in partnership with John Lock, the lord of the manor. Between them they owned the *Nautilus*, a 48-ton vessel, which brought coal and lime into Lynmouth and very occasionally took some cured herrings to Bristol.

Thomas Baker gradually came to realize that the old farming and fishing economy was in decline and that the new opportunities were in tourism. In 1841 he

An 1873 advertisement for the Royal Castle Hotel.

The Royal Castle Hotel in 1859. Fine views could be obtained from the terrace.

purchased the Castle Hotel from Dr John Clarke, a wealthy Lynton landowner. It was then that he showed his business acumen, greatly improving the hotel and attracting both the rich and the famous. He also operated the Lynton to Minehead coach, a service which brought many visitors to his hotel.

In October 1856 Thomas Baker's hotel received the ultimate accolade of a royal visit. The fourteen-year-old Albert Edward, Prince of Wales, travelled with his tutor by train to Barnstaple, and then hired a light carriage to travel on to Lynton for a two-night stay at the Castle Hotel. Although the visit was supposed to be an incognito one it received widespread publicity. Mr Baker subsequently renamed his hotel the Royal Castle Hotel and in his advertising boasted that the young prince had stayed there.

Yet, despite his success as a hotelier, Thomas Baker never gave up his links with the old way of life. He still owned a farm and specialised in rearing Exmoor ponies. Up to the age of 70 he rode in the front rank of the huntsmen following the Devon and Somerset staghounds.

Thomas Baker played a major role in the life of the community, serving as churchwarden to four vicars at the parish church and holding the office of parish clerk for nearly 50 years. He was also a long-serving member of the Local Board and a leading member of the National School committee.

At times he could seem very hard. In April 1868 he had a ten-year-old boy called John Sharp sent to Barnstaple gaol on suspicion of setting fire to his hay rick. This boy was too poor to go to school, so Thomas Baker had employed him on his farm and had himself given the boy matches to burn gorse. After five days in custody the boy's case was heard before

Thomas Baker is the old man holding a walking stick in this posed photograph taken c.1886. Charles Medway, a butcher, sits in the centre of the stocks with Thomas Prideaux, a blacksmith, on his left. The man in the top hat is J.Colwill, a member of the Ilfracombe family who operated a coach service to Lynton.

the magistrates and he was discharged.

Thomas Baker was not a man to cross for he fiercely criticised those he disliked. In 1881 he wrote a letter to the *Lynton and Lynmouth Recorder* describing Giles Jose, a fellow-member of the Local Board, as an 'insignificant puppy of a tailor' and implying that Jose had been obliged to return from the colonies because of the crimes he had committed there. In 1888 he was threatened with a libel case when he had a letter published in the same newspaper which described Major Hunter, a leading pillar of Lynton society, as 'dreaded by all and better-known than

trusted'.

Thomas Baker had no time for new-fangled ways. He described the 1880 Act which brought in compulsory education as an 'abominable law'. In a letter to the *Lynton and Lynmouth Recorder* he declared:

I have known many boys of this parish who earned their own living at the age of eight or nine and when men commanded the best ships out of London and Bristol. Since the later mode of education has been established, scarcely one boy has turned out worth a rope.

The Lynton Cottage in the early twentieth century. The Sanfords had sold the property to Sir Charles Smith in 1860. Thomas Baker purchased it in 1870 and his son then ran it as a private hotel.

Yet, although he could be hard, he was intensely loyal to those he considered his friends. We shall see that when the Revd Lawson came under fierce attack from most of his parishioners, it was Thomas Baker who, as vicar's churchwarden, fiercely defended the beleaguered clergyman.

As an old man Thomas Baker often reminisced about the days when Lynton and Lynmouth had been a remote farming and fishing community, inaccessible to the wheeled vehicle and served only by one church. 'I can remember the time when there was not one dissenter or a pair of common cartwheels in this poor parish', he was fond of saying. He was an important link with the past and his death in January 1890, at the age of 86, seemed to many to mark the end of an era.

THOMAS HEWITT (1837-1923)

Thomas Hewitt was born at Lichfield in 1837. His family were members of the Warwickshire gentry and no money was spared in giving him a good education. After passing his law examinations in 1864, Thomas at first practised as a solicitor in London. It was, though, as a barrister specialising in taxation that he was to make his mark. Soon he was acknowledged as the leading expert in

Sir Thomas and Lady Hewitt electioneering in Cornwall in 1906. He stood as a Liberal Unionist for Camborne, but was unsuccessful in a Socialist stronghold.

cases involving income tax. In 1899 he was appointed a Queen's Counsel and in 1904 he was honoured with a knighthood. He also had commercial interests, being chairman of an insurance company and director of a property company.

His first marriage began with high expectations but ended in tragedy. The wedding bells peeled out in April 1864, yet sadly only thirteen months later his bride was dead. In the family records Thomas wrote just one word: 'Alas'. His wife had gone to an early grave, but had left a baby daughter to be brought up by a nanny.

In September 1869 Thomas married again and this time was blessed with happiness. His seventeen-year-old bride was Fanny Powles of Eastwood Park in Yorkshire. Horses were Fanny's great love so Tom planned an adventurous honeymoon riding on Exmoor. This was how they came to make their first visit to Lynton and Lynmouth.

Seldom does a man have the chance to love a woman and a view at the same time but that was to be Thomas's good fortune. Hand in hand they were strolling along North Walk admiring the fine views of Lynmouth Bay. Suddenly Thomas stopped and asked his young bride: 'Would you like to live here?' She looked puzzled. Thomas picked up a stone, marked it and asked her to throw it down the slope. 'Wherever it lands we shall have a house built,' he declared.

He was as good as his word. The stone had landed on a rocky slope which

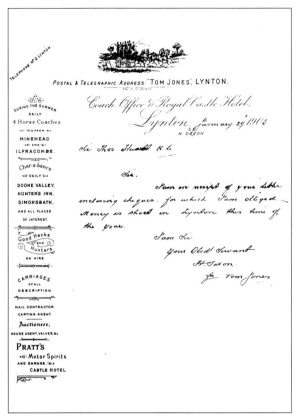

The local tradespeople depended on the gentry for much of their trade. Note the telephone number and the varied activities undertaken by Tom Jones's business.

seemed quite unsuitable for a house, but before long a site was being dynamited out of the cliff. A grand house was to be erected there with a terrace and a magnificent sea view. They named it the Hoe.

Each summer they would leave London behind and spend several weeks at their cliff-side residence, entertaining distinguished friends. Here their three sons would spend many happy holidays and in later years return with their wives.

Thomas Hewitt was big in every sense of the word. Bearded, six-foot-three in height, he had a powerful presence. Possessing a keen brain and a caustic tongue, he was not a man to cross.

Servants held him in awe. Lynton councillors and tradespeople were constantly chivvied when he felt he was not receiving the service he expected. Yet he was a fair man who commanded respect. His youngest son Peter described him as 'just and extraordinarily straightforward'.

Thomas insisted on a fixed ritual at the Hoe. All the family had to be dressed and at table for breakfast by the time he sat down. The sons knew that they would be refused a meal if they arrived late. On more than one occasion they crept out to buy breakfast in one of the hotels.

Only the butler and principal servants were to be seen doing their jobs. Junior staff were expected to be unobtrusive, except at morning prayers when the whole household had to assemble to hear Fanny take a short service.

Thomas occasionally liked to remind the locals that he was an important personage. So, when in his later life he had occasion to travel to London, he would wait until the train was about to leave Lynton station and then have his butler phone the station and ask them to hold the train. As he was a director they could hardly refuse!

In the 1880s Thomas Hewitt promoted a scheme for a pier which, if it had been built, would have enabled a flood of trippers to be landed at Lynmouth. Yet, in later years, Thomas became obsessed with the need to keep up the social tone. In an era when the common man could at last afford to travel, he did all that he could to prevent excursionists reaching the select resort.

Imagine his fury when from time to time they trespassed on his property. On one occasion a party of five trippers mistook the Hoe for a hotel, went down

Copley Hewitt, Thomas Hewitt's second son, married Alice Woolsey, an American, at Beaulieu Abbey. They came to Lynton for their honeymoon.

the drive, rang the bell and asked for lunch. The butler thought that they were expected guests, arriving early, and served them a sumptuous meal. The error was only discovered when the intruders called for the bill at just the moment that the family arrived back.

When Thomas was at home his sons had to 'toe the line', but when he was away on business things were very different. One summer Peter, the youngest son, had a tutor down to coach him for the finals he had to sit at Greenwich College, before becoming a naval officer. Taking advantage of his father's absence,

Copley Hewitt and his new wife arrive at the Town Hall during their marriage celebrations. The carriage was pulled by lifeboat men, wearing their cork jackets. The Lynton Band played.

CELEBRATIONS
AT LYNTON
On Saturday, Oct. 14th 1905
IN HONOUR OF
THE MARRIAGE
OF
Mr. COP. HEWITT,
(Son of Sir Thos. and Lady Hewitt, of The Hoe.)

1.30 p.m.	Lynmouth School Children (and friends), headed by the TOWN BAND, will meet opposite Lynmouth Church and proceed to the Cliff Railway for Lynton.
2. 0 p.m.	**PROCESSION** From top of Cliff Railway to National School to join Lynton and Barbrook Mill School Children (and friends) proceeding then to a Field adjoining Cottage Hospital, kindly lent by Mr. J. Stanbury.
3. 0 p.m.	**TEA FOR CHILDREN.**
4. 0 p.m.	**Refreshments for All,** SPORTS (under the direction of Mr. W. H. Northcott.) **GAMES. DANCING.**
6. 0 p.m.	**FIREWORKS** BY MR. WILLIAM PALMER.
7.30 p.m.	SELECTIONS by BAND on Town Hall Balcony.
8. 0 p.m.	**VARIETY ENTERTAINMENT** at the **TOWN HALL** By Ladies and Gentlemen of the neighbourhood, assisted by Mr. D. E. Calthrop and Mr. Harry Rice.

Lady Hewitt, in the large hat, and her lace-making class outside the Hoe, c.1909.

Sir Thomas and Lady Hewitt on the terrace at the Hoe in the summer of 1912, with Rowena, wife of their youngest son Peter, and her baby Mary Diana.

Sir Thomas and Lady Hewitt watching a game of tennis on the court high above North Walk, c.1912. On the court, left to right, are Peter, Rowena, Alice and Copley.

Peter sent for the German band, which was performing in the resort. Every morning he had the band play for him as he studied on the terrace. Having no money to hand, he rewarded their efforts with the fine claret, port and sherry he had discovered in his father's cellar. The bandsmen were delighted with the arrangement!

Fanny Hewitt was rather overshadowed by her husband, but she was a dutiful wife with a strong social conscience. It was Fanny who paid, from her private purse, to have some fine cottages erected at Lynbridge for the use of the deserving poor. Fanny was also concerned at the lack of winter employment for local women and brought in an expert to teach them the skills of lace-making. All visitors to the Hoe were expected to buy some of the lace her classes produced.

Fanny was with Thomas when he died. One January day in 1923 the old man retired after lunch to his study. Fanny helped him into his chair and realised that his life was slipping away. One kiss on the forehead and he was gone. A strong personality, he was one of the last of a dying breed of gentlemen who had brought both money and gentility to the resort.

A Glut of Schools and Churches

THE Revd William Lawson was appointed Perpetual Curate of Lynton in 1866. Never before or since has the parish had such a controversial priest. He would spark off bitter disputes over both religion and education. Many would oppose him, and as a result new churches and schools would mushroom in a quite remarkable way. Seldom can a parish have witnessed

Entrance to Lynton in the early 1860s. At this time conditions in the village were still primitive. Part of the old Valley of Rocks Hotel can be seen beyond the Church.

such competition to minister to the minds and souls of its inhabitants.

The Revd Lawson took over a parish in which the Church of England was dominant. There were Nonconformists in the parish, but they formed only a relatively small minority. Not until 1835 had the Nonconformists opened a chapel in Lynton, on Lydiate Lane (now a house known as Mole End). In 1850 they had replaced it with a Congregational chapel (near the bottom of Sinai Hill). This chapel had only had modest support from the locals. Most had continued to worship at the parish church. Relations between the two churches had usually been good.

In educational matters the Anglicans had nearly always had a virtual monopoly. In 1818 the Revd Charles Kekewich, the parson, had founded a school and in 1820 he had affiliated it to the National Society for Promoting the Education of the Poor, which was a Church of England organization. His National School had briefly faced competition when in 1831 John Mortlock had started a small Nonconformist infant school. This wealthy china-dealer had taken up residence in a cottage facing the church and had started holding services there. Yet after a few years his school had closed. The National School had flourished and had moved to new premises by the Crown Hotel in 1844. For many years it had had no real rivals, apart from two small private schools which catered for only a handful of children.

So with no real religious and educational conflict before his arrival, how was it that the Revd Lawson soon managed to upset so many of his parishioners? Certainly his brand of Anglo-Catholicism offended many. This was a period when many Englishmen were hostile towards Roman Catholicism.

The Crown Hotel, 1859. The Congregational Chapel can be seen to the right. It was built in 1850.

Some Lynton worshippers thought that the new parson's services included far too much ritual and smacked of 'popery'. His abrasive manner also upset people. All too frequently, the vestry meetings ended with the Revd Lawson sweeping out in a rage, taking the parish minute book with him to prevent all further discussion.

One particularly stormy confrontation took place when the Revd Lawson had only been in the parish for a few months. In December 1866 he called the inhabitants to a vestry meeting, to discuss his proposals for restoring the parish church. These included removing the old private pews and replacing them with chairs, and building a large new chancel. The parishioners had already made it clear that they were firmly against the changes.

The Revd Lawson opened the meeting by talking of 'an Evil Spirit who must be wrestled with'. Then to everyone's surprise he suddenly pointed to John Clarke, the local doctor, and said that he was this evil spirit. There was uproar! When the Revd Lawson's scheme was put to the meeting it was roundly defeated.

In the following week the Revd Lawson

Left: The controversial reredos, c.1870.

called another meeting in the hope of overturning the decision. After a heated debate, his resolution to go ahead with the restoration failed even to obtain a seconder. The *North Devon Journal* reported: 'Everyone stood up and amidst a scene of cheers, waving of hats and shouting of congratulations ... the meeting terminated'.

The Revd Lawson had suffered a defeat, but he still insisted on the need to have the church restored. In 1868 the parishioners decided that, for the sake of peace, they would allow him to go ahead with his scheme.

The restoration was completed and in June 1869 Bishop Trower arrived to consecrate the new chancel. As the congregation filed in for the service, all eyes turned towards the new chancel, and particularly towards the new reredos, an ornamental stone screen backing the altar. Everyone was shocked to see sculptured religious figures on this reredos. These effigies had been placed there without the knowledge or consent of either the bishop or the parishioners. The people were upset and angry.

The resulting battle over the reredos hit the headlines. Pressure mounted for the removal of the figures, partly because some objected to what they claimed were 'graven images', and partly because others were upset at the 'clandestine manner' in which they had been installed.

In December 1870 the parishioners voted to apply for a faculty to remove the 'objectionable figures from the reredos'. The case was heard before the bishop's Consistorial Court in Exeter in April 1871. William Riddell, the parishioners' churchwarden, represented the inhabitants, and Thomas Baker, the parson's churchwarden, represented the Revd Lawson. After a lengthy hearing the Revd Lawson was ordered to remove the offending effigies.

When Mr Riddell returned to his home at Lynmouth he was greeted with flags, flowers and gunfire. Then he was presented with an address signed by the heads of many leading families. In short he was treated like a conquering hero.

When the Revd Lawson arrived back in Lynton, he too was given a great welcome. It was stage-managed by Thomas Baker, his loyal churchwarden. The church bells were set ringing. A band met the parson and led him through the town. Children from the National School lined the streets and threw garlands. Finally a crowd gathered to enjoy an open-air tea paid for by Thomas Baker.

Yet nothing could hide the fact that the Revd Lawson had suffered a major defeat. Late one night he went to the church and removed the offending figures. He covered the empty niche with black velvet.

The reredos controversy had serious repercussions. Most locals now regarded their parson as a 'papist' and thought he could not be trusted. Some boycotted his services. Many parents decided that they

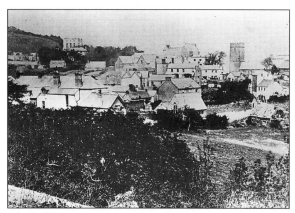

Lynton, c.1879. The National School can be seen in the foreground. The ruined cottage to the right of the school may be the remains of the old parsonage. On the hill to the left is Summit Castle.

St John the Baptist Church can be seen in this late nineteenth-century view of Lynmouth.

did not want their children exposed to his religious instruction in the National School. Such was the depth of feeling that some leading local people began to consider opening new churches and schools that were not under the parson's control.

Mr Whitehead, a Yorkshire mill owner who had recently taken up residence at Rock House, was responsible for the founding of the first new church. After seeing the new reredos in 1869, Mr Whitehead realized that he could no longer stomach the Revd Lawson's brand of religion. At once he decided to establish a Free Church of England church in Lynmouth. Services were held in a first-floor room of a building which also housed a coal cellar and a marine store. A minister was appointed and given a generous stipend.

In October 1870 Mr Whitehead opened the Lynmouth Free Church School in the same upper room. To save on costs he appointed as mistress Mary Lane, a 20-year-old teacher without a certificate. This school was always a small one. In October 1873 it had 11 boys, 16 girls and 18 infants. All were taught in a room measuring only 38 feet by 36 feet. Mr Whitehead died in 1871 but his wife continued to give financial support to both the church and school.

The Revd Lawson was not prepared to surrender Lynmouth to a rival church, so he decided to have an official Church of England church erected in the village. In August 1871 he conducted the first service at St John the Baptist Church. He must have wondered whether to rejoice that the Church of England at last had a place of worship in Lynmouth, or whether to grieve that there were two competing churches in what was still only a small village. Later in the decade a Plymouth Brethren chapel also opened at Lynmouth, making the rivalry even more intense.

The Revd Lawson's unpopularity also led to a new place of worship opening in the hamlet of Barbrook. Early in 1870 a small group of locals, being 'offended by the ritualism introduced into the parish church', decided to invite some Methodists from Barnstaple to come and lead services in a private house at Barbrook. So many local people attended that the decision was soon taken to build

Looking up Watersmeet Road in the 1880s. St John the Baptist Church, Lynmouth is on the left. Bonnicott is on the right.

a Wesleyan chapel. The new Barbrook Wesleyan Chapel opened in June 1871. So large was the crowd that the first services had to be held in a meadow.

Then in January 1872 the Wesleyans opened a school in a large ground-floor room of their Barbrook chapel. Richard Veall, a certificated teacher, was appointed master. He wrote in the log book: 'Opened school on Monday with 19 scholars. Many of them have been accustomed to read only from the Bible and consequently stumble over many of the words in an ordinary reading book … Find that it will be necessary to enforce strict discipline'. This master set a high standard and his school was soon highly regarded.

The National School also faced new competition in Lynton itself. It was on 22 May 1871 that Charles Collins, an experienced teacher, wrote in his diary: 'Began school in two rooms in an old farmhouse with 18 scholars' (the site now occupied by Palmer's Dairy). This school was run by the Congregationalists.

The Congregationalists were able to open this new school because they were receiving financial backing from Isaiah Jupe. This wealthy gentleman lived at Mere in Wiltshire and owned a large silk mill there. In the 1860s he had met the daughter of William Collard, a keen Nonconformist residing at Combe Park. After marrying her at the Congregational chapel in Lynton, he had decided to fund the Congregational cause in the parish.

In 1871 Isaiah Jupe bought Croft Place

Barbrook in the 1890s. The Wesleyan Chapel and School can be seen on the right. A small schoolmaster's house is attached.

on Lydiate Lane (now Sylvia House Hotel and Croft Cottage). He used the two houses to accommodate his school master and the Congregational minister. The former chapel in the grounds, which for many years had been used as a coach house, was converted into a schoolroom. The school moved there in the following year.

This school was soon affiliated to the British and Foreign School Society, which sponsored Nonconformist schools, so it was known as the British School. The school flourished and drew many children away from the National School. By 1873 it had on roll 20 boys, 14 girls and 29 infants.

On his visit to the parish in 1873 the School Inspector was astonished to find so many schools. In addition to the Lynton National School, the Lynton British School, the Lynmouth Free Church School and the Barbrook Wesleyan School, he discovered that there was also a small private school run by a Richard Huxtable and a dame school run by a Mary Comers. So, quite remarkably, there were no less than six schools in competition. This in a parish where there were at most 210 children of school age, not all of whom could afford to attend school. The competition was fierce, not least because each school derived part of its income from the weekly coppers parents had to pay to send a child to school.

The National School was hit hard. Many pupils were lost to new rivals, so the income from school pence decreased. As the number of pupils declined, so too did the grant from the Government. At the same time the school lost the backing of many former subscribers. The Revd Lawson must have felt everyone was against him. He saw both the Lynmouth Free Church School and the Lynton British School receiving generous financial aid from wealthy patrons, while most of the local farmers were switching their support from the National School to the Barbrook Wesleyan School.

The parson decided drastic action was needed. In May 1873 he shocked the parish by announcing that his National School would close due to lack of funds. Some sympathised with him in his financial predicament. Many thought he was trying to force them to make more donations towards a school they disliked.

The Revd Lawson knew that while the 1870 Education Act had not made education compulsory, it had decreed that all children should have the right to go to school. Those districts lacking an adequate number of voluntary schools were compelled to open non-denominational schools, which were to be paid for by compulsory rates. These new schools were to be administered by boards of elected members and hence would be known as board schools.

William Lawson knew that, apart from his National School, the Barbrook Wesleyan School was the only school in the parish that was recognized as efficient, and he was well aware that that school was far too small to accommodate all the children of school age. So he was giving his parishioners a choice. Either back his church school or face the heavy expense of building and running a board school. Fear of religious indoctrination coupled with threats to the pocket; this was a mix guaranteed to whip up feeling.

His tactics misfired. At a public meeting the majority of parishioners made it clear

that they still would not support the Lynton National School, but nor did they want the expense of a board school. They promised the Department of Education that much needed improvements would be made to the Lynton British and Lynmouth Free Church Schools. After long deliberations the Department of Education decided that these two schools plus the Barbrook Wesleyan School could between them fill the gap left by the closure of the National School.

So the Revd Lawson's bluff had been called, and he was horrified to find that the education of the children was to be left in the hands of those he described as 'Dissenters'. He soon had his National

LYNTON NATIONAL SCHOOL.

The above School has been Re-opened, after the Christmas Holiday, and now takes its place as a School under Government Inspection. The Services of a Certified Master (trained at S. Mark's College, London), and his Sister, have been secured.

The School, though a Church of England School, will be conducted under the Conscience Clause, and according to the requirements of the Government New Code.

SUBJECTS TO BE TAUGHT :—READING and SPELLING, WRITING, ARITHMETIC, HISTORY, ENGLISH GRAMMAR, GEOGRAPHY, ANIMAL PHYSIOLOGY, PHYSICAL GEOGRAPHY, and DRAWING, including FREE-HAND, MODEL, GEOMETRICAL, and PERSPECTIVE.

Fees for Standards I. II. III.   ..   .. 2d. per week.
   "   Standards IV. V. VI   ..   4d.   "
   " Day-school Hours : 9 to 12 a.m.—2 to 4.30 p.m."

The Sunday School commences at 9.30 a.m. and at 2.30 p.m.

The Managers earnestly request the Parents of the School Children to help them by seeing that their Children *Attend Regularly*, and in good time, and that they learn their home lessons properly.

The necessity for a Higher Class School, in connection with the Lynton National School, has been brought under the notice of the Managers, and is now receiving their consideration.

W. L. LAWSON,

VICAR OF LYNTON,

For the Managers of the Lynton National School.

Epiphany, 1874.

Printed by R. A. LAWRENCE, at the "Herald" Steam Printing Works.

The National School was reopened in 1874. Note that parents had to pay to send their children to school.

Lee Road, 1911. The Wesleyan Church beyond the Town Hall had replaced the little chapel on Blackmore's Path.

School open again. Once more he began pleading for subscriptions from visitors and residents.

The vicar had suffered yet another setback but he was far from beaten. At Easter 1876 he once again announced the closure of his National School. He declared that it would stay shut until the parishioners agreed to support it by paying a voluntary rate. He warned that their only alternative was to form a school board and pay a compulsory rate. He felt confident of winning, for he knew that the promised improvements at the rival schools had not been made.

The closure of the Lynton National School left over 70 children looking for a new school to attend. This time the School Inspector decided that the cramped accommodation at the Lyn-

mouth Free Church School was quite unsuitable for an increased number of pupils. In April 1876 a letter was sent to Mrs Whitehead stating that the Education Department would not recognize her school unless the lighting was improved, the room furnished with proper desks and also that 'convenient privies' were provided. Mrs Whitehead's response was swift. She closed her school. This left another 20 children with no place of education.

Those opposed to the Revd Lawson were now in a tight corner. In June 1876 the parish received a Final Notice from the Education Department stating that, unless school accommodation was provided for a further 90 children within six months, then the parish would be required to open a board school.

Many parishioners were still determined neither to give in to the Revd Lawson's demand for a voluntary rate nor to agree to having a board school. At a public meeting they resolved to build and manage a new school at Lynmouth which would be 'free from sectarian teaching'. Those present agreed to back it with voluntary contributions.

On 20 March 1877 the new Parish School opened at Middleham, Lynmouth, thus removing the threat of a board school. The *North Devon Journal* rejoiced that the 'entire control of the school was in the hands of the inhabitants' and education in the parish was 'no longer the plaything of priests'.

The Revd Lawson was not a man to admit defeat. As soon as he realized that his scheme had been thwarted, he once again reopened his National School. Many local people were furious.

Competition between the churches was also intensifying. In 1875 the Revd Lawson opened a Mission Chapel at Barbrook, hoping to win back worshippers from the Wesleyan chapel. Many thought it absurd to have two places of worship competing in a small hamlet. In 1880 the Wesleyans hit back by opening a chapel in Lynton (the building is now used as a Masonic Hall). At Lynmouth Mrs Whitehead decided that her Free Church of England church needed bigger premises, and so in 1877 she rehoused it in an iron church that she had erected beside the river near to Rock House.

Rarely can such a small number of people have been so well supplied with places of worship. Whereas before 1870 there had been only two churches in the parish of Lynton, ten years later the population of some 1,200 had a choice of eight churches or chapels. This meant that there was a place of worship for every 150 souls!

Competition between schools also increased still further. In 1877 the Revd Lawson announced that he planned to open a new school in his Mission Chapel at Barbrook. This was a mischief-making proposal, for there were only a handful of children living in the Barbrook area, and the Wesleyan School amply met their needs.

The parson's first step was to build a school teacher's house next to the chapel. Then in November 1877 he advised the

BARBROOK-MILL

ORPHANAGE FOR GIRLS,

AND

NATIONAL SCHOOL.

LYNTON PARISH, NORTH DEVON

Patron:
THE RIGHT REVEREND THE LORD BISHOP OF EXETER.

Ladies' Committee:
LADY M. AUGUSTA ONSLOW,   MRS. LAWSON,
LADY DENISON,   MRS. EDMONDS,
LADY NELTHORPE,   MRS. LUXMOORE,
MRS. FOSTER-MELLIAR,   MISS WALKER.

Local Committee:
THE RURAL DEAN OF SHERWILL,
THE LICENSED CLERGY AND CHURCHWARDENS OF
LYNTON PARISH.

Chaplain and Secretary:
REV. W. L. LAWSON, M.A., VICAR OF LYNTON.

Honorary Medical Adviser:
CHARLES HARTLEY, ESQ., M.R.C.S., LYNTON.

Treasurer:
THE MANAGER, NATIONAL PROVINCIAL BANK, BARNSTAPLE.

———————

The chief objects of the promoters of this little Orphanage and National School are—
(1) To give food, raiment, and sound religious and secular education to a few little girls who have lost one or both parents, and to train them for domestic service;
(2) To provide, at a small cost, the advantages of National School Education, under a trained and certificated Mistress, for those girls and infants of Barbrook Mill and the neighbouring hamlets, whose parents may desire it, by utilizing, to the fullest extent, the little Mission Church adjoining the Orphanage, which is fitted up with reversible school desks, and a moveable screen separating the Chancel from the body thereof.
The Mission Church was dedicated and licensed for Divine Service on S. Bartholomew's Day, 1875, when the Ven. the Archdeacon of Barnstaple preached. Every Sunday since that date the Church has been used for the

Part of a pamphlet about the Barbrook Orphanage and National School, 1879.

Department of Education of his intention to open a school and applied for a Government grant. An inspector reported that the application was 'purely vexatious'. It was turned down.

Far from being deterred, the Revd Lawson came up with another way of funding his school. He decided to use the new teacher's house as a small orphanage, and to charge fees for placing children in

Barbrook, c.1900. Between 1879 and 1882 there was a small orphanage in the house and the Barbrook National School used the Mission Chapel.

it. These orphans he then planned to use to swell the numbers of children in his school, in the hope that this would persuade the Education Department to give the school a grant.

In January 1879 the Barbrook National School and Barbrook Orphanage both opened. Mrs Ridge, a certificated teacher, was put in charge of the two establishments. By March the school had attracted about 20 pupils and there were three small girls living in the orphanage with the teacher.

Yet on 9 June 1882 the Revd Lawson wrote to the National Society: 'I beg to inform you that the Barbrook National School is now closed and I do not see any way to reopen it'.

Why had the school and the orphanage been so hurriedly closed? Press reports and comments hint at the answer. In August 1882 a letter in the *Lynton and Lynmouth Recorder* indignantly declared

One of the Revd Lawson's many fundraising efforts.

that the 'mistress some months back, being in a disgraceful condition, left suddenly without any satisfactory explanation'. It was also reported that the parson had had to go abroad because of ill health, leaving curates in charge of the parish. Another letter to the same paper referred darkly to 'the circumstances in which Mr Lawson undertook to leave Lynton and never return as vicar'.

In the years that the Revd Lawson was absent on leave, the strife gradually died down. The curates he left in charge were

A class at Lynton National School, c.1895.

much more moderate men. They succeeded in healing most of the divisions which had split the community.

The changed spirit was soon in evidence. In 1880 local people had willingly shouldered the burden of keeping the British School open, after Mr Jupe had been forced to withdraw his support due to financial problems at his mill. Yet in December 1884, with the parson away from the parish, the managers had no qualms about closing the school. They were even happy to recommend to parents that Lynton children should transfer to the Lynton National School. Then in January 1886 Mrs Whitehead announced that she would be removing her iron church to Combe Martin. There was no longer the same need for it at Lynmouth.

Late in 1886 William Lawson announced his resignation. He returned to Lynton and made a farewell speech. In it he referred to the 'vexations, disappointments and buffetings' that he said he had experienced during the 20 years of his ministry. He admitted that 'not all that he had done had been perfect', but, as he pointed out, 'no one was'. He also called attention to his achievements in the twenty years he had been incumbent. Significantly, these had all been built of stone and mortar. Building works he would long be remembered for, but sadly he had had very little success in constructing good relationships with his parishioners.

It was to be left to his successor to rebuild bridges between parson and flock. In January 1887 the Revd Walter Eustace

The new Convent, 1911. It was opened on Lee Road in 1910, the same year as the Wesleyan Church.

Rear view of the Convent, c.1910. This view shows the piecemeal development that was taking place. Streets
were being laid out, but only a few houses at a time were being built.

Cox preached his first sermons. The *North Devon Herald* said it hoped he would 'promote peace, concord and good will'. This he was to do most ably. With a much-loved parson in control, there were no more quarrels over churches and schools. Yet it was many years before the parishioners forgot the controversies that had marked the Revd Lawson's time in the village.

The new spirit of tolerance was shown in 1904 when most people welcomed the arrival of a group of Roman Catholic nuns in the parish. These nuns were members of the order of St Clare and came from France. Changes in their own country had caused them to leave for England. Father Hugh Lean, a Roman Catholic priest and a member of a local landowning family, had taken pity on the nuns and had rented Prospect House at Lynmouth for them.

Father Lean then decided that these Poor Clares should be permanently housed in a convent at Lynton. The cost of this expensive project was met by wealthy English Catholics. Father Lean personally paid for a church to be built next to the convent, even though he knew that, apart from the nuns, there were only five Catholics living in the parish. The convent and church on Lee Road were opened in September 1910. The fact that this Roman Catholic presence was so readily accepted in Lynton and Lynmouth showed that the days of serious religious conflict had come to an end.

'The Healthiest Spot in the Country'

'THERE is no place in England so healthy,' declared Dr Thomas Cooper in his 1853 guide to Lynton and Lynmouth. Such outrageous claims were not uncommon. Since the 1750s doctors at the South Devon resorts had been asserting that their pure sea water and mild maritime air was a certain cure for a whole range of life-threatening diseases. It was much more difficult for a small centre on the exposed north-facing Bristol Channel coast to develop a reputation as a health resort, but this Lynton doctor was determined to do his best to attract potential patients.

In his book Dr Cooper made his case by emphasising the 'rare purity of the air' at Lynton and Lynmouth. He claimed that the resort was remarkably free from all contagious diseases and stated that 'amongst the natives of Lynton a death from consumption is extremely rare'. As a final proof of the resort's salubrity, he drew attention to the 'extreme age which almost all the inhabitants attain'. He must have been finding it difficult to make a living, for he wryly concluded: 'A surgeon can neither live nor die in it, so healthy is it'.

Sea-water cures were in vogue, with many seaside doctors boasting of miraculous recoveries through bathing in the sea. Lynmouth was not noted as a bathing resort, but this did not stop Dr Cooper drawing attention to the advantages it had for those who wanted a dip in the sea. He announced: 'A machine for bathing in the sea was a few years since built by subscription' and was 'entrusted to the bathing women for the use of visitors'.

At bigger resorts on the Devon coast bathing machines had long been a familiar sight. For almost a hundred years these large wooden boxes on wheels had been protecting modesty. They were used to shield bathers from prying eyes while changing and then being trundled down to the sea, where attendants would dip them under the waves. Now Lynmouth could boast the same facility.

Dr Cooper might also have mentioned that hot and cold sea-water baths were available for the sick and infirm, and indeed for all who wanted to obtain the benefits of the healing brine without being buffeted by icy waves. This was an amenity that all Devon resorts felt obliged to provide once their clientele was large enough to justify the capital outlay.

As early as 1830 it had been reported that Lynmouth had a 'bath-house lately erected, of neat appearance, where hot

The west beach in the early 1860s. Bathing machines can be seen.

and cold baths are prepared'. This was a building with a classical façade which stood on the site of the present Bath Hotel. About 1832 a short tower was erected on the jetty, from which sea water was supplied to the bath-house. Some people complained that the squat structure on the jetty was an eyesore, so in or about 1850 General Rawdon, the owner of

Lynmouth, c.1836. The short tower can be seen on the jetty. Walking from there along the riverside you would come to the first Lyndale Hotel, then to a house and then to the bath-house, the building with a classical façade.

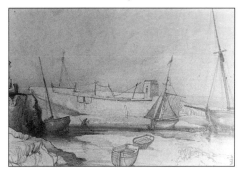

Right: The jetty in 1835. This detail from a pencil drawing shows the squat tower.

Lynmouth, c.1853. Henry Trix's establishment is the building on the far right.

Clooneavin, had a more attractive top added, giving it the appearance of a Rhenish tower. By 1838 sea-water baths could also be obtained at Henry Trix's establishment by the harbour (now Seabreeze Cottage).

In his book Dr Cooper claimed that Lynton and Lynmouth had none of the sanitary problems that beset so many inland towns. He emphasised the purity of the drinking water, claiming that it was 'free from the slightest impregnation of earthy matter'. He also pointed to the 'abundance of running water … to flush away the sewers constantly and to wash away all refuse matter so prejudicial to health as well as to the olfactory nerves'. Dr Cooper was well aware that at Ilfracombe in 1849 the lack of an adequate sewerage system had brought about a serious outbreak of cholera, so he could not resist pointing out: 'Whilst the cholera was raging in Ilfracombe and every other watering place around, Lynton and Lynmouth stood pre-eminent, for not a case occurred here'.

It was certainly true that at the time of the 1849 epidemic some of Ilfracombe's visitors had fled in terror to Lynton and Lynmouth. Yet while they dare not admit it for fear of driving away the visitors, the inhabitants were concerned about the sanitary state of their resort. In 1854, less than a year after Dr Cooper had praised Lynton and Lynmouth's sewerage system in his guide, the local Medical Officer informed the Lynton Vestry that the main drain through the resort was 'defective both in size and form'. His report was prompted by news that a new cholera epidemic threatened England. There was talk of a new sewerage system, but once the danger receded the proposals were soon forgotten.

In 1866 a new cholera epidemic swept the country. Soon it reached both Bristol and Swansea. This time Lyntonians really feared both for their lives and their livings. They knew that there was a grave risk that visitors arriving by sea from those ports would bring the disease with them. While they wouldn't publicly admit it, they were aware that the insanitary conditions in their resort were an ideal breeding ground for cholera. If cholera arrived they knew it would decimate the local population and drive away the visitors.

The ratepayers held a series of public meetings at which all agreed that major sanitary improvements were needed. Yet they also reached the conclusion that under the fragmented system of local government then prevailing in the district, it would be impossible to initiate a comprehensive public-health scheme. It was pointed out that while some aspects of local administration were conducted by the ratepayers at their Vestry meetings, sewering improvements were the prerogative of the Barnstaple Poor Law Union, and the roads under which pipes would have to be laid had become the responsibility of the new Ilfracombe Highway Board.

Lynmouth from the jetty, c.1847. The bath-house can be seen on the right, beyond the woman and child.

The inhabitants decided that the time had come for them to take full control of their own affairs and they resolved to seek the independent powers of a Local Board. This was an unusual step for a small township with a population of only just over a thousand. The Government normally only sanctioned the granting of Local Board status to districts with over three thousand inhabitants. Special reasons had to be advanced: Lynton and Lynmouth argued that as it was a resort 'much frequented by visitors', but with 'imperfect drainage and many nuisances', it urgently needed greater powers so that it could initiate major sanitary improvements. The Secretary of State agreed and in December gave his formal sanction to the application.

The Local Board's first priority was to provide a completely new sewerage system. The existing drainage of the resort was totally unsatisfactory. Some of the sewage was flowing along open drains into cesspits near the centre of Lynton, some trickled along pipes into the East and West Lyn. Yet the capital cost of installing new sewers under all the streets and then transporting the sewage out to the sea seemed daunting for a small watering place with relatively few ratepayers. The solution arrived at was to have the project supervised by John Litson, a Lynmouth surveyor, who knew the resort well but worked for only a small fee, and to insist that he kept to a tight budget. Progress was swift. By May 1867 the work of laying sewers under the streets was nearly complete and an outfall was being constructed so the sewage could flow into Lynmouth Bay. In October 1868 a Government inspector reported that the works were 'well and substantially constructed' for the very moderate outlay of £750.

The inhabitants recognised that an improved water supply was just as urgent a need. Lynton's existing supply originated from the Ladywell Spring just outside the resort, but it flowed through meadows where 'cattle delighted to wallow in the water' and then ran in an open chute, passing 'unpleasantly close' to a privy. Finally, it arrived at some catch pits near the Valley of Rocks Hotel, from where the people had to collect their needs. Lynmouth's water was drawn partly from a spring on Mars Hill and partly from the polluted East and West Lyn. Yet while there was general agreement on the vital need for improvements, there was a problem about paying for them, for the new Local Board was already faced with having to raise a substantial rate to pay for the new sewerage scheme.

Lynton and Lynmouth therefore welcomed the offer by a group of prominent residents to form a private company to supply piped water. The water was to be brought from a new source at Cherrybridge on a tributary of the West Lyn. The directors of the company included Robert Roe and Dr John Clarke, two leading landowners. Thomas Baker, the proprietor of the Royal Castle Hotel, and John Crook, owner of the Valley of Rocks Hotel, were also directors. All these men were undoubtedly motivated by a genuine desire to safeguard the health of their fellow villagers. Yet they also had a financial interest in protecting the resort's reputation as a healthy place to holiday in. The landowners hoped to be able to sell building sites at advantageous prices, while the hotel proprietors wanted to ensure that their hotels were well filled with wealthy visitors.

The work of providing Lynton and Lynmouth with a piped supply commenced early in 1867. By October sufficient progress had been made for Robert Roe, the Chairman of the Water Company, to be asked to officiate at a ceremony to mark the turning on of Lynton's water supply. He stood in front of the Valley of Rocks Hotel, hose-pipe in hand:

> He waited some time and no water came. He then had a look at the mouth of the hose, when suddenly the water came with such force that it knocked off Mr Roe's hat, the water going clean over the hotel roof.

Perhaps this mishap was a portent of the problems that would eventually bedevil the water supply.

In 1873 many of the residents banded together to raise the funds to build a cottage hospital in Lynton. Charles Frederick Bailey of Lee Abbey was the chief promoter of the scheme, but others also subscribed. James Lean, a local landowner, generously leased the land for a token rent of only a shilling a year. Building stone was given free of charge and local farmers volunteered to transport it.

Situated on Lee Lane (now Lee Road), the Cottage Hospital was the first substantial building to be erected in the meadows to the west of the old village. This hospital was originally intended to meet the needs of the poor people of the parish and neighbourhood. It opened without ceremony on 18 May 1874 with the admission of two female patients. Ever

Lynton from Hollerday Hill, c.1880. The hospital stands alone in the fields.

Fields still extend up to the hospital. On the opposite side of the road is the Wesleyan Church which was opened in 1910. The hospital extension has not been built so this photograph must be before 1922.

since then it has given valued service to the community.

In the 1880s alarming rumours began to circulate about the quality of the water being supplied to residents. In February 1887 the *Lynton and Lynmouth Recorder* brought the issue out into the open with a report that the tank on Sinai Hill, which held the filtered water, contained 'muck as high as a man's knees besides numerous fish'. It was also claimed that small fish were finding their way down the pipes to the customers' taps.

There were also complaints about the unreliable nature of the supply. In August 1890, at the height of the holiday season, the Company's small reservoir was unable to meet the demand and it was reported that 'lodging-house keepers were running hither and thither in search of water'. Feelings ran high about a company which had just paid its shareholders a ten per cent dividend, but failed to adequately supply the resort.

While the inhabitants had at first been content to see the waterworks in private hands, they now began to agitate for public control of this important utility. When the Company had been set up in 1866 with a capital of £1,000, 162 of the 200 shares had been subscribed for by Lyntonians. This had meant that the waterworks had been under the control of local people who were answerable to their fellow citizens. But by the 1870s most of the shares in the Company had been bought up by a group of Barnstaple businessmen. The inhabitants resented outsiders taking over the company, particularly when these people seemed more interested in making large profits than in improving the quality and reliability of the water supply. As early as 1876 the Local Board had made an offer of £3,500 for the Company, but the bid had been flatly rejected.

Demands for public control of the waterworks steadily mounted. They reached a peak in November 1890 when the Water Company announced its intention to seek an Act of Parliament giving it powers to construct a larger reservoir, and also guaranteeing it the exclusive right to supply the resort in the future. The Local Board resolved to oppose the Bill on the grounds that control of water should be in the hands of the inhabitants rather than a company 'engaged in the undertaking merely as a trading venture for profit'. In March 1891 a Select Committee of the House of Lords spent four days taking evidence before deciding to reject the Company's Bill. It was thus established that the Company had no exclusive right to supply the resort with water. Almost at once the Local Board proposed bringing in its own supply of water from an intake on the Furzehill branch of the West Lyn. This seems to have been a ploy to force the Company to sell out, for at the same time the Board offered £2,400 for the entire enterprise. This figure was flatly rejected.

With deadlock reached, the Lynton Board applied to the Government for sanction to bring its own supply of water. At the same time the Company again sought an Act of Parliament, this time to enable them to raise additional capital so that they could obtain more water from a new source further upstream. It was the prospect of further heavy legal costs which finally forced the parties to negotiate and in December 1892 the Local Board finally acquired the waterworks on a long lease.

Once the waterworks was safely back in local hands, some of the enthusiasm for

*Councillors and officials of the Lynton Urban
District Council in 1919.*

an expensive new project evaporated. Several schemes were looked at by the Lynton Urban District Council, which under the reorganisation of local government succeeded the Local Board in 1895, but it was only in 1903 that the decision was taken to construct a new waterworks. Cost considerations ruled out plans for a higher intake, so the Council decided to retain the existing one at Cherrybridge, though with a much improved filtration scheme. Pressure was increased by supplying the town directly from the intake instead of via the old reservoir on Sinai Hill. This meant that

water could be supplied to a height 50 feet above that previously reached, an important consideration for a resort surrounded by hills and short of building sites. In June 1904 Sir George Newnes was asked to perform the opening ceremony. This was a surprising choice for his mansion on Hollerday Hill was the only house the new supply could not reach.

As proof of the healthy state of the resort, the Urban District Council in 1900 produced a publicity leaflet boasting that in the previous year it had a 'phenomenal death-rate of 9.7 per thousand'. To our generation it seems strange to find a resort boasting of its low death-rate, but this was a health-conscious age. Prospective visitors wanted proof that watering places were not ravaged by disease, so resorts often tried to produce lower death-rate statistics than their competitors, just as they now vie to top the sunshine league table. The figure claimed for Lynton and Lynmouth was certainly a remarkably low one when compared with a national death-rate of 18.9 per thousand.

Almost half a century earlier Dr Cooper had been emphasising the therapeutic qualities of the pure air and water. Now the local authority was giving at least some of the credit to its sanitary achievements. It was certainly trying to promote Lynton and Lynmouth's claim to be a health resort. The leaflet trumpeted that it was 'the healthiest spot in the country'.

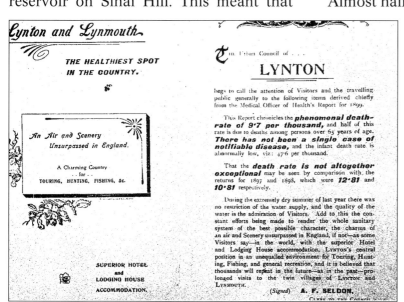

Publicity leaflet published by the Council in 1900.

George Newnes

(1851-1910)

NEVER in Lynton and Lynmouth's long history has so much been owed to one man. From the moment George Newnes first set foot in the town, he played a leading part in its development. He spent freely, exerted enormous influence and brought about major changes.

George Newnes was born at Matlock Bath in Derbyshire in 1851. The third son of a Congregational minister, he was sent to boarding school at the tender age of nine. In his early years he displayed no enthusiasm for learning and was something of a disappointment to his parents. The Revd Newnes had hoped that George would follow him into the ministry, but it soon became clear that George had no desire to become a clergyman.

When George was fifteen his father arranged for him to be apprenticed to a fancy-goods merchant in London. There he showed real initiative and when only seventeen was put in charge of a large department. Recognizing his potential, the company sent him to Lancashire to open a new branch. He married Priscilla Hillyard, the daughter of a Congregational minister, and they settled in Manchester.

One evening in 1880, while sitting at home thumbing through the pages of the *Manchester Evening News*, George Newnes found an item of really interesting news in what was otherwise a rather dull read. After studying this story he exclaimed to his wife: 'That's what I call a real tit-bit. Why cannot a paper be brought out containing nothing but tit-bits similar to this?' George turned the idea over and over in his mind. He was well aware that, as a consequence of the

George and Priscilla Newnes.

Outside George Newnes' mansion at Putney Heath. George Newnes is in the rear seat and his son Frank holds the steering wheel. Frank gained a reputation as a reckless driver after he once reached a speed of 40 m.p.h.

Education Act of 1870, most of the younger generation of working men and women could read. The more he thought about it, the more certain he was that the time was ripe for a cheap, entertaining and easy-to-read magazine aimed at the mass market.

How could the capital be found to publish such a magazine? With no one prepared to lend him the money, George rented a disused cellar and in a short space of time turned it into a flourishing vegetarian restaurant. Mr Newnes' brother-in-law later told how he went looking for George and found him, not in the vegetarian eating house, but in a nearby hotel tucking into a beefsteak.

'Everyone to his own fancy!' said George with just the hint of a wink. After only a few weeks the restaurant was sold at a handsome profit, providing the money needed to launch a new magazine.

On Saturday, 22 October 1881 George Newnes took the plunge and published the first number of *Tit-Bits*. Newspaper boys were sent out onto the streets of Manchester with the penny magazine. Two hours later they returned to the office where George sat anxiously waiting. They brought good news. They had sold some 5,000 copies.

George Newnes soon gave up his job with the fancy-goods company and put all his energies into editing and publishing his magazine. Snippets of interesting information were gleaned from a wide range of books and periodicals. He had a flair for publicity: free insurance cover was given to anyone who had a railway accident while carrying a copy of *Tit-Bits*; a villa named 'Tit Bits' was offered as a prize to the reader who contributed the best short story; clues to the location of a tube of gold sovereigns were given in the magazine. Circulation soared. Within two years it had reached 200,000. Up and up it climbed until eventually it reached 850,000.

Success followed success. He launched *The Review of Reviews* and the *Strand Magazine* and both periodicals soon had a huge readership. Other journals followed close behind. Then he began to produce a large range of cheap books aimed at the working man. George Newnes was building up a publishing empire.

Soon he branched out into other forms of business. Everything he touched seemed to turn to gold. He was, for example, quick to see the financial opportunities offered by the development of the internal combustion engine and he became a major shareholder in the French Daracq motor-car company.

George Newnes had become a celebrity. He had a magnificent house built at Putney Heath. In 1885 he was invited to stand in the General Election as the Liberal candidate for Newmarket. He triumphed against all the odds in this former Tory stronghold and was elected to Parliament with a majority of 973. In the New Year's Honours of 1895 his services in politics and in the cause of popular literature were acknowledged when he was awarded a baronetcy.

'I work hard and I play hard,' George

declared. In his spare time he was often to be found on a golf course or enjoying a game of tennis. He was also a keen chess player and was made president of the newly formed British Chess Club.

It was through chess that George Newnes came to know Thomas Hewitt, for Thomas Hewitt was vice-president of the same club. It was at the invitation of Thomas Hewitt that in September 1887 George and Priscilla Newnes and their two young sons made their first visit to Lynton, staying with Mr and Mrs Hewitt at the Hoe.

This was to be the first of many holidays in Lynton and Lynmouth, for George Newnes found that there he could relax and for a time cast off the pressures of business. Often on his early visits he would hire the Manor House, or another large gentleman's residence, for the summer months.

Late in 1890 George Newnes decided to purchase Hollerday Hill and build his own summer residence there. At first sight this hill seemed an unlikely site for a mansion, for its steep, windswept slopes seemed bleak and uninviting, while the thin, stony soil hardly supported a single tree. Yet he realised that a house there would afford panoramic views, while, with careful planning, the slopes surrounding the house could be converted into wooded grounds of rare beauty.

The first step was to construct an approach road to the site. In May 1891 Messrs Jones Bros. started the difficult task of cutting a road out of the rocky hillside. George Newnes' love of animals led him to insist on a winding route so that horses did not suffer unduly on the climb.

In October 1892 work commenced on the building of the mansion. Teams of

The workmen who built Hollerday House.

horses were kept busy hauling heavy loads of both Bath and native stone up to

Hollerday House. George Newnes had the trees planted.

the site. A small army of local workmen were employed for many months. By the end of 1893 the mansion had been completed.

George Newnes never tired of the enchanting views to be had from Hollerday Hill, but he was a big-hearted man who liked to share his good fortune. In a typically unselfish gesture he opened Hollerday Hill to the general public, stipulating only that visitors would not pick the ferns and other rare plants that he had had planted.

Later chapters will show that George Newnes invested large sums in commercial ventures at Lynton and Lynmouth, putting up much of the capital for both the Cliff Railway and the Lynton and Barnstaple Railway, and going to the considerable expense of obtaining an Act to build a pier. Yet after deciding to become a resident he helped to preserve the resort's exclusive character, first by

Lynton and Lynmouth, c.1894. George Newnes' new mansion stands high on Hollerday Hill.

abandoning his pier scheme and then by opposing proposals for railways from both Filleigh and Minehead, fearing that they would open the resort to the 'common crowd'.

George Newnes also made a number of generous gifts to the town and locality. In 1891 he paid for Warren Field in the Valley of Rocks to be levelled for a cricket ground, and then arranged to have a cricket pavilion erected there. In May 1894 he performed the opening ceremony at the new golf course on Martinhoe Common, which he had helped to pay for. Before long he would announce his intention to make a much more substantial gift to the local community.

For some time there had been complaints that the town lacked the quality of public building normally expected of a fashionable watering place. Public meetings usually took place in the Foresters' Hall, which stood next to the Crown Hotel. The Lynton Local Board and the Lynton Urban District Council, which succeeded it in 1895, had been obliged to hold their meetings in rented rooms. Early in 1897 the Councillors considered purchasing a cottage in front of the Crown Hotel, with the intention of converting it into a small council room and office. There was opposition from those who objected to the ratepayers' money being spent in this way. Other

Lynbridge early in the twentieth century. The saw mill can be seen in the valley.

residents opposed the proposal for a quite different reason. They felt that the town needed a much more prestigious building. They launched a fund-raising scheme with a view to erecting a proper town hall, as a way of commemorating the Diamond Jubilee of Queen Victoria. This proved far too ambitious a plan for such a small community and it fell through due to lack of support.

On an October day in 1897, the Councillors were holding their monthly meeting in a rented room at Gordon Villas when Bob Jones, the builder, hurried in bearing remarkable news. He announced that he had received a telegram from Sir George Newnes. The message read: 'If not too late, attend the Council Meeting and explain my scheme for a public hall'. Bob Jones told the astonished Councillors that

he had sold Sir George a plot of land on Lee Road, and that Sir George proposed having a magnificent Town Hall erected on the site as a gift to the community.

11 May 1898 was certainly a red-letter day in the history of Lynton and Lynmouth. After Lady Newnes had officially opened the Lynton and Barnstaple Railway, the party of dignitaries arrived on Lee Road where a large crowd watched Lady Newnes and Mrs Jeune, lady of the manor of Lynton, lay the foundation stones for the new building.

The Town Hall took two years to build and cost £20,000. Jones Bros. obtained the contract and the building bears testimony to the skills of the company's craftsmen. Much local stone and oak was used in the construction. The timber was sawn at the water-powered mill at

Opening of the Town Hall, August 1900.

Lynbridge. The architects, Messrs Read and Macdonald of London, cleverly married elements of the English manorial, Gothic and Tudor traditions, so ensuring that, instead of being formal and pompous, the Town Hall would provide refreshing variety. In short, the building displayed the popular 'pick-and-mix' formula that had proved so successful in *Tit-Bits*.

On 15 August 1900 Sir George Newnes performed the opening ceremony. After unlocking the main door with a silver key, he formally handed over the building to the town, expressing the hope that it would be 'a source of instruction and recreative pleasure, not only to the present inhabitants, but to future generations'. This it has certainly proved to be.

Sir George was to make yet another magnificent gift. For many years the Congregationalists in Lynton had been hampered by the small size and inconvenient position of their chapel on Sinai Hill. When first opened in 1850 this chapel had been close to the centre of the old village, but in the 1890s it had found itself left behind in a quiet backwater, after the town had begun to expand towards the Valley of Rocks. Bob Jones was a member of the local congregation

Lee Road, August 1904. The Revd R.J.Campbell and Sir George Newnes leaving the Congregational Church after an opening service.

and in 1903 he offered to give a building plot for a new church on Lee Road, the street which was fast becoming the main thoroughfare. The small congregation realised that it would find it difficult to raise the money for such an expensive project, so that August they decided to approach Sir George to see if he would make a donation towards the cost. His response exceeded all expectations. He offered to triple the size of the site, and as a memorial to his father he said that he would also meet all the costs of constructing a much grander church than had originally been contemplated. Needless to say the offer was gratefully accepted. Bob Jones was once again awarded the building contract. The new church was opened for worship in August 1904. The Revd R.J.Campbell, a famous London preacher, took the opening services. George Newnes was later to make him a present of a new car.

Elsewhere in England Sir George was

also giving away large sums on schemes to benefit the public. At Matlock, his birthplace, he provided an electric tramway; at Putney he provided a fine Free Library; in London he gave a considerable sum to the Salvation Army. He also found money to fund scientific research, in 1898 providing £38,000 to make possible an expedition to the Antarctic.

George Newnes was a national figure who brought prestige and excitement to a small provincial resort. He was greatly respected in the town. Each summer, the arrival of the Newnes family became an occasion for rejoicing, with flags flying and cannon sometimes being fired. Lynton often had cause to celebrate in his era. On major days, such as the opening of the Lynton and Barnstaple Railway, the houses were decked with flags and bunting; floral arches were suspended across the streets; bands played and the people joined long processions through the twin villages.

The greatest festivities were reserved for the coming of age of Frank, the only surviving son of Sir George and Lady Newnes. On a September day in 1897 the Royal North Devon Hussars Band led a long procession through the town and up to Hollerday House. There Frank was presented with a silver salver from the inhabitants. The procession then returned to a field near the hospital, where over 2,000 people were given a sumptuous dinner of turkey, goose, duck, beef and ham. In the evening Hollerday Hill was illuminated with no fewer than 14,000 coloured lights. The evening climaxed with a magnificent display of fireworks followed by the firing of a huge bonfire. This was a day which lived long in local memories. George Newnes was much

Frank Newnes receiving a silver salver from the townspeople at the celebrations to mark his coming of age.

moved by the genuine affection shown by the local people. He said that it was one of the happiest days of his life. It was hardly a coincidence that later that month he offered to provide Lynton and Lynmouth with the Town Hall.

The rich and the famous came to visit him. In September 1902, for example, Sir Arthur Conan Doyle was entertained at Hollerday House. This famous author knew Sir George well, for his Sherlock Holmes stories were published in Newnes' *Strand Magazine*. He made the main speech when a life-size marble bust of Sir George was unveiled at the Town Hall.

Yet George and Priscilla Newnes experienced times of sadness as well as joy. At the age of seven their younger son Arthur died from 'brain fever'. George Newnes was only forty, but he aged overnight and his fair hair soon turned grey.

He also experienced a serious setback in his political career. In 1895 he lost his Newmarket seat. He was bitterly disappointed and, although he was at once offered three safer seats, he decided

Summit Castle. George Newnes purchased this old lodging-house and in 1904 had it raised to the ground to improve the views from his property. This sketch shows it in 1847.

Sir George Newnes towards the end of his life. He was only fifty-nine when he died.

that for the time being he would retire from active politics.

While he was staying at Hollerday House in September 1900 a deputation arrived from Swansea, asking him to stand as the Liberal candidate in the forthcoming Parliamentary election. He agreed and promised to go to Swansea the very next day, as the election was only ten days off. A tugboat was sent to collect him, but the sea was rough and it was unable to put into Lynmouth. Sir George sent a message: 'Will come tomorrow even if I have to swim!' Cross the Bristol Channel he did, even though the storm still raged. After a whirlwind campaign, Sir George captured the seat from the Tories with a majority of 1,114.

Life in Lynton and Lynmouth was never dull when Sir George was in residence. In August 1905 his magnificent new yacht steamed into Lynmouth Bay for the first time. The *Albion* was thought to be the largest and best fitted-out private yacht in England. Needless to say its presence in the bay caused great excitement. Early in September Sir George left on his yacht to visit his constituency in Wales.

A few days later Lynton's first-ever bowling match was due to be played. Sir

George had acquired the old lodging-house known as Summit Castle, which stood immediately below his Hollerday grounds. The site had been cleared to improve his view and a fine new bowling green had been made there. Sir George had invited a club from Barnstaple to play a local team in the opening match. A splendid pre-match lunch at the Castle Hotel was drawing to a close and still there was no sign of Sir George. Then, from the windows of the hotel, the *Albion* was sighted. Sir George hurried ashore and was just in time to attend the opening ceremony at his new green.

Sadly in his last years Sir George was dogged by financial problems. Always he had been confident of his ability to make more and more money to replace that which he spent so lavishly, but now this gift deserted him. Some of his investments began to lose money and new speculations proved disastrous.

Business worries began to affect his health. He lost his sparkle and retreated into himself. His doctor diagnosed diabetes, but to those who knew him well it seemed as if he was losing his zest for

Hollerday House on the morning after the fire.

life. Slowly his strength began to ebb away. In the summer of 1909 his doctor advised that he needed to rest. When he arrived in Lynton to take a long holiday it was obvious that he was a sick man. He was to spend the last months of his life at Hollerday House.

Problems mounted. In August 1909 it was announced that the profits of his flagship company, George Newnes Ltd, had plummeted due to increased competition in the magazine business. Then in January 1910 came the news that in the General Election Frank Newnes had lost the seat he had held for four years as M.P. for Bassetlaw in Nottinghamshire. Sir George took great pride in his son and this sad blow hastened his end. Occasionally that spring Sir George was still to be seen taking a few steps on Hollerday Hill, but as his end drew near he had to be carried out onto the terrace in front of his house. It was at Hollerday House he died one morning in early June. At the request of Lady Newnes, her husband was buried at the top of the cemetery in Lee Road, as close as possible to the hill he loved so much.

A certain magic went out of local life with the passing of George Newnes. Lyntonians had felt they were living in his reflected glory; they had taken pride in his many achievements and they had marvelled at the wealthy and fashionable visitors he had brought to their little resort. He had made them a free gift of splendid public buildings and had greatly improved transport facilities. He had also given the resort a 'golden age' when it prospered as never before or since. The locals had good cause to mourn his passing.

When Sir George's will was published it was clear that most of the family fortune had gone. His son Frank was to spend most of his life paying back the debts his father had left.

Lady Newnes and Frank shut up Hollerday House, said their goodbyes and left the town. Lyntonians pleaded with them to return but never again were they to summer at the resort. Money had to be found to pay off debts and before long Hollerday House was on the market. The furniture was disposed of at auction but the house stood empty, for no one would meet the asking price.

At eleven o'clock on the night of 4 August 1913 a series of explosions were heard. Flames were seen pouring out of the empty house. By the time the Lynton fire brigade arrived the house was well ablaze. The firemen found that the pump that brought water to the tank supplying the house was out of action. Eventually they brought in their own supply from down in the town, only to find that the pressure of water was inadequate for their needs. It soon became clear that nothing could be done to save the house. By morning the interior had been largely destroyed.

Everyone agreed that the fire was the

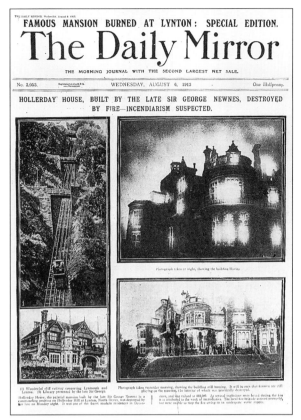

The fire made the headlines in the national papers.

work of arsonists, but who was to blame? Sir Thomas Hewitt had no doubts. He declared it to be the work of suffragettes but there was no evidence to support his claim. The fire was a mystery. What was clear was that Lynton had lost an imposing building and with it many memories of its greatest resident.

The Cliff Railway

ONE of the main obstacles to the development of Lynton and Lynmouth was the 450-feet-high cliff which separated them. For centuries, long lines of packhorses had had to toil up the hill carrying coal, lime and the many necessities of life which were brought into Lynmouth by sea.

The almost sheer cliff was a major problem when the tourist industry developed. The steep gradients placed enormous strains on the ponies and donkeys, hired at 6d. a time to carry visitors between Lynmouth and Lynton. The horses which were used to pull carts and coaches up the hill to Lynton likewise had a very short life.

In 1881 Major Hunter of Rock Lodge suggested to the Local Board that a new road, with less steep gradients, should be constructed between Lynmouth and Lynton. It was a good idea, but there was never any real chance of his scheme being adopted, for it involved using part of the Glen Lyn estate. The owner of Glen Lyn was William Riddell, a retired solicitor and and also a leading figure in the community, and he used his considerable influence to scotch it.

The proposal, however, did prompt a much more original suggestion for solving the problem of moving passengers and freight up and down the cliff. In December 1881 the *Lynton and Lynmouth Recorder* received a letter, signed only with the nom-de-plume *Pro Bono Publico*, proposing:

A tramway between the two towns to be worked by a stationary engine at Lynton, the motive power being taken from the river Lyn, put in tanks on rolling carriages and these let down the tramway under proper control. The weight of the water going down would, with the application of simple machinery, bring up anything that might be desired from Lynmouth.

Such a novel scheme would be a great tourist attraction. It captured the imagination of the local people, but at first no one was prepared to put up any capital so it was nothing more than a talking point.

It was late in 1885 that a major project was proposed which included the building of a cliff railway. There were three parts to the scheme. Firstly, the construction of a solid pier extending 112 yards into the sea, from a point some 930 yards north-west of Lynmouth Harbour. This was intended to enable Lynmouth to attract a bigger share of the growing steamer-excursion traffic. Secondly, the building of a promenade providing access to the pier, from a point near the Rhenish Tower. Thirdly, a 'lift from the said pier or promenade to Lynton'. This was to make possible the speedy movement up to Lynton of the large numbers of people, it

The Cliff Railway under construction, c.1889. Note the deep scar on the hillside. The bridges have still to be built.

was hoped would be landed from the steamers at the new pier.

Thomas Hewitt and John Heywood were the co-promoters of this ambitious proposal and both hoped to make fat profits from it. At first sight they were ill-matched. Thomas Hewitt was a gentleman from London. John Heywood was a local tradesman who had started as a humble grocer and had prospered sufficiently to

The Cliff Railway, 1890.

have opened the Bath Hotel at Lynmouth.

Yet on closer examination it was apparent that together they were well-equipped to see the scheme through to a successful conclusion. Thomas Hewitt had the legal skills and influence to guide the Bill through Parliament. John Heywood had the local clout. He had become both the Chairman and Treasurer of the Lynton Local Board, an unusual and highly irregular combination of positions which gave him considerable power.

As his part of the arrangement Thomas Hewitt did all the legal work. The Bill came before Parliament in March 1886 and by October the Lynmouth Prom-

Left: The Cliff Railway just prior to opening, 1890. George Newnes is on the left, Bob Jones, the engineer, stands between him and the driver.

The stop on North Walk in 1911. The Cliff Railway made it easier for visitors from Lynmouth to reach this walk.

enade, Pier and Lift Provisional Order had received official sanction.

As his part of the agreement John Heywood promoted the project in Lynton and Lynmouth. Even though he had a financial interest, he still used his influence to persuade the Local Board to spend ratepayers' money in assisting the scheme, and in so doing reduced the investment his company would have to make. At the monthly meeting of the Local Board in January 1886 he proposed the following motion: 'That it is desirable to improve the condition of Lynmouth Beach and to construct a short esplanade

Right: Cliff Railway in use, c.1890.

North Walk in 1908. The original entrance to the Hoe can be seen on the right.

for the convenience and comfort of visitors'. These were the official reasons for the building of a promenade but not the real one. Members of the Local Board were told of an unofficial understanding with the promoters. It had been agreed that if the Local Board built an esplanade running 165 yards westwards from the Rhenish Tower, then the private company would extend the esplanade and build a pier at the end of it. The members agreed to have plans drawn up and then to consider the matter further.

The idea that ratepayers should shoulder the heavy financial burden of an esplanade met with a mixed reception in the resort. Many of the tradespeople gave the scheme their enthusiastic support, for they believed that a pier would bring great prosperity to the resort. Those without a financial interest in the tourist industry were strongly opposed to the idea that

ratepayers should have to dip into their pockets to help a private venture.

After a year of debating this controversial scheme, the Local Board met in January 1887 to decide whether to give the final go-ahead. Ratepayers were excluded from the meeting. The majority of the Local Board members were local businessmen and they voted by six votes to three to go ahead with the building of the first part of the esplanade.

The Local Board opened their esplanade in September 1887, but John Heywood and Thomas Hewitt never kept their part of the bargain. Their company built neither the pier, nor the esplanade extension, nor the lift. Many of the local inhabitants felt cheated!

What made John Heywood and Thomas Hewitt abandon their plans? In part it may have been the insistence by the steamer companies on a longer pier than

Beach House and beyond it the Bath Hotel, c.1900. As early as 1878 John Heywood was running a small hotel in the house which stood next to the bath-house. Between 1878 and 1881 he extended this hotel three times, taking in the site previously occupied by the bath-house.

the one proposed, so that steamers could come alongside it at low tide. This would have added substantially to the construction costs.

Their change of mind may also have been brought about by the loss of the Portishead steamers. As we have seen, the Great Western Railway stopped this service late in 1886 and in 1887 there were far fewer visitors arriving by sea. Local businessmen grew ever louder in their demands for a pier, knowing that it would encourage more excursion steamers to call. Yet, while a pier would have undoubtedly led to a substantial increase in the number of sea-borne day trippers, the loss of the only regular

passenger steamer service must have made John Heywood and Thomas Hewitt question whether the revenue from tolls on the pier and fares on a cliff railway would ever be sufficient to return a profit on their investment.

It was just at the time when the pier and lift scheme was foundering that George Newnes made his first visit to the resort. Early in September 1887, he and his wife were invited to spend a few weeks as the guests of Thomas Hewitt at the Hoe. It is just possible that Thomas Hewitt invited George Newnes in the hope that his rich friend would agree to take over the project.

Arriving by carriage, George Newnes

was shocked to see 'horses almost falling under their burdens' climbing Lynmouth Hill. Once at the Hoe he raised the matter. Thomas Hewitt explained that he himself had included proposals for a lift in his pier scheme, but there was little likelihood of it being built, because of the large capital investment required.

'Is there any one in the place capable of constructing such a railway?' George Newnes asked. Yes there was such a man, he was told: Bob Jones, a skilled engineer and a partner in Jones Bros., the local builders who were just completing the construction of the esplanade.

With his customary eagerness, George Newnes asked that Bob Jones be asked to call the following evening. He later wrote of his first meeting with this engineer: 'That night we fixed up a plan by which we could make a cliff railway. I took the rest in hand'.

This was the way George worked. He saw an opportunity and took it. Schemes which met a public need and at the same time made him a profit appealed to him. He was quick to realise that the novelty of a cliff railway would draw in many new visitors and might restore local prosperity, while at the same time providing him with a good return on his investment. He agreed to put up most of the capital, but Bob Jones and Thomas Hewitt also invested money in the project, and eventually became his fellow directors.

Less than a fortnight later the *North Devon Herald* reported: 'A meeting of the Pier and Lift Company has just been held to decide whether they should construct the lift, or whether they should accept the offer of Messrs Jones Bros. to construct it and carry it on at their own responsibility and risk. Finally the latter course was

decided upon and excavations are being made'.

The newspaper stated that the water was to be drawn from the West Lyn at Lynbridge. It also reported that the lift would start from the esplanade just being completed at Lynmouth, and that it would rise to a point on North Walk where it would be met by the footpath called Wester Way.

Construction was delayed. First there were disputes with those who owned the land over which it was proposed to make the railway. Then there were legal objections from Mr Riddell of Glen Lyn, who feared that the extraction of water from the West Lyn would have a detrimental effect on the waterfalls in his grounds. Eventually, in 1888, the promoters of the Cliff Railway were obliged to go to the considerable expense of obtaining an Act of Parliament to give them the powers they needed to construct their lift without obstruction.

Although the Promenade, Pier and Lift Company which John Heywood had helped set up had relinquished the right to construct the lift, he was still to play an important part in the events leading to its construction. As Chairman of the Local Board and a public-spirited member of the community he was striving to bring greater prosperity to the resort. Yet it is clear that he was also an astute businessman who was seizing every opportunity to make a profit.

In his private capacity as a business speculator, John Heywood had already acquired the lime kilns and all the gardens and fields bordering the route of the new esplanade, that in his public capacity as Chairman of the Local Board he had persuaded his fellow members to build at public expense. Once this esplanade was

Valley of Rocks Hotel, c.1880. Later in the 1880s the part on the left was demolished to make room for a large extension. On the extreme left is part of the Church.

local businessman. He believed that the value of the hotel he had just bought would be enhanced by having the cliff railway terminate by it.

completed these sites had considerable potential for development, and it was clear that they would increase in value even more if a cliff railway was to come down to them. So in April 1888 John Heywood agreed, in consideration of an annual payment of £80 a year, to lease out some of his land at Lynmouth, so that the track for the lift could pass over it on its way down to the new esplanade. In doing so he made certain that the bottom terminus of the Cliff Railway would adjoin land he owned.

John Heywood also took steps to make sure that the top terminus of the cliff railway would likewise be next to land he owned. In the spring of 1888 he purchased the Valley of Rocks Hotel. He at once made it possible for the cliff railway to construct both their top station and the approach road to it on land which had been part of the grounds of this hotel.

This can be viewed as a public-spirited action by a respected local man. By enabling the cliff railway to travel to a point much higher up the cliff, he had removed the need for passengers to have to toil up North Walk Hill. Instead they could walk from the terminus along a level road into the town. His action can also be regarded as a shrewd move by a

Having made sure that he owned the prime sites at both the top and the bottom of the railway, John Heywood was soon making plans to develop them. In April 1888 the *Lynton and Lynmouth Recorder* announced that at the end of the season the old part of the Valley of Rocks Hotel would be demolished and a splendid new wing would be built there. The same newspaper also reported that at Lynmouth the lime kilns would shortly be demolished to make room for a new hotel.

John Heywood was not a rich man and he needed capital to pay for such large developments. Knowing that the Valley of Rocks Hotel and his land along the esplanade had increased substantially in value, since he had ensured that they would be served by the cliff railway, he decided to raise some money on them. He did this by selling these properties at a handsome profit to a new company he founded, called the Lynton and Lynmouth Hotel and Property Company. John Heywood received £36,000 from the wealthy businessmen who bought shares in it. He remained a major shareholder in the new company and was its managing director.

By the beginning of 1890 the cliff railway was almost complete. In February

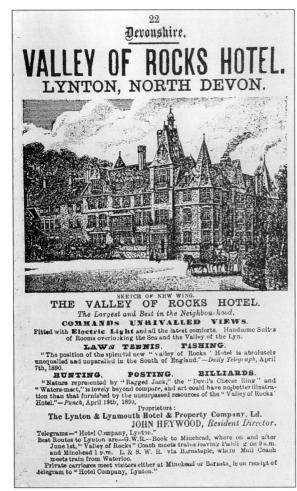

This guidebook advertisement for 1892 lists the facilities at this greatly enlarged hotel. The new wing can be seen on the right.

The interior of the Valley of Rocks Hotel in 1907.

Jones Bros. announced that they had successfully used it to transport a load of cement from the harbour to their Lynton store, the first of many heavy cargoes brought in by sea and moved up to Lynton in this way.

As the opening day approached an air of expectation gripped the twin villages. Most of the inhabitants looked forward to an era of great prosperity. Only a few people grumbled about the 'scar on the face of the cliff' caused by the major excavations that had taken place.

The Cliff Railway finally opened on Easter Monday 1890. Passenger cars began moving up and down the cliff and the twin villages rejoiced. Floral arches decked the streets. One at Lynmouth declared 'Now we want a pier!'

At a special luncheon held in the magnificent new wing of the Valley of Rocks Hotel, George Newnes cheered many local hearts when he announced that he would give 'every possible assistance' in realising the resort's fondest dream: the provision of a deep-water landing pier. Perhaps he was prompted by the fact that that morning the steamer *Waverley* had arrived in the bay with a party of excursionists. They had come to ride on his new cliff railway, but had been prevented from landing by the rough seas.

If, in addition to the esplanade and cliff railway, a pier had been built, it would have completed a trio of major developments which would have turned the sedate and select resort of Lynton and Lynmouth into a mecca for sea-borne day trippers. A later chapter will explain why George Newnes eventually had second thoughts, and went back on his promise to build the pier that the business community so badly wanted.

New Lamps for Old

I N THE SAME week that the Cliff Railway was officially opened, in April 1890, the Electric Light Company began supplying the resort with electricity. Once again it was water that was put to work, this time to provide energy for a hydro-electric power station on the East Lyn.

The founder of the Electric Light Company was Charles Geen. Born at Lynmouth in 1840, he was a son of Thomas Geen. As a young man, Charles had gone off to Okehampton to make his own way in the world. There he had built up a large building firm with workshops and warehouses. As early as 1880 he had harnessed the waters of the East Ockment River to generate electricity for use in his works. Charles had been joined in business by his brother Henry and in 1889 they had begun to supply electricity to light the streets of Okehampton. They were pioneers, for Okehampton was the first town in the West Country to have the new form of lighting.

Charles Geen knew that Lynton and Lynmouth badly needed an improved system of lighting. Gas lighting had been proposed in 1875 by the Local Board, but there had been a storm of protests. Objectors had pointed out that the proposed gas works at Middleham would disfigure the scenery, pollute the air, damage the fishing and drive away the visitors. The opposition had been led by Mr Halliday of Glenthorne, supported by Lord Tenterden, a brother-in-law of Mr Bailey of Lee

The Electricity Power Station in 1899.

Abbey. In the face of such powerful opposition the Local Board had backed down. So Lynton and Lynmouth was one of the few resorts without gas lighting. Oil lamps were used in houses and to illuminate the streets.

Charles Geen was also aware that the East Lyn came down steeply from the hills and had the potential to generate enormous power. He had the skills to build a hydro-electricity works and he knew that there would be a considerable demand in the booming resort. So he decided to construct a generating station in the valley above Lynmouth.

Early in April 1890 the first electric lights were switched on. By the end of the month the Local Board had scrapped most of its old oil lamps and was illuminating the principal streets with electric lights. Businessmen were also quick to take advantage of the new supply. They were soon announcing that their hotels and shops had the new lights.

At a time when electricity supply was still in its infancy, the resort had become one of the first in the country to have this fashionable new form of illumination. It was also one of the few resorts without smoke pollution from a gas works or a coal-fired electricity works. Lynton and Lynmouth had left the 'Dark Ages' and its bright lights symbolised its new determination to be in the vanguard of progress.

Boom and Bust

ALL the heady talk of landing piers and a cliff railway triggered off a development boom unprecedented in Lynton and Lynmouth's history. Excitement ran high in the period between 1886 and 1892. The inhabitants were convinced that, once the twin villages were made more accessible, a golden era of great prosperity would follow. Businessmen spent heavily on land and property. New buildings mushroomed on all sides. After years of stagnation the resort began to expand outside its old boundaries. Yet the boom would come to a sudden end, leaving some people facing ruin.

William Bevan, the owner of the Lyndale Hotel at Lynmouth, was the first to make a substantial new investment. He leased the whole of the Tors estate from the lady of the manor. Then in July 1886 he opened the magnificent new Tors Hotel on a prime site overlooking Lynmouth Bay. At the end of that year he began advertising 'fifty splendid building sites in Tors Park all commanding uninterrupted sea and land views'. His advertisement claimed: 'Villas and houses are in great demand now that it is decided to bring the railroad into Lynton and a new pier at Lynmouth'.

Other major hotel developments soon followed. In July 1887 the Kensington Boarding House (now the Imperial) was opened by John Holman, who was already the proprietor of the Queen's Hotel. In the same month John Crook opened a handsome extension to his Valley of Rocks Hotel. In 1889, after the Valley of Rocks Hotel had been taken over by the Lynton and Lynmouth Hotel and Property Company, work began to completely demolish the old part of

Left: William Bevan began as a mason and became a successful businessman. In 1880 he purchased the Lyndale Hotel from Miss Jones. He built the Tors Hotel in 1886 and the Lyn Valley Hotel in 1895. Above: Staff at the Lyndale Hotel, 1886.

Lyndale Hotel, c.1890. This hotel was damaged in the flood disaster of 1952 and was subsequently demolished. The Lyndale car-park now occupies the site.

The Tors Hotel, c.1900.

Church Hill House and the old part of the Valley of Rocks Hotel, c.1880.

the hotel. Soon a new wing was being erected. It had spacious bedrooms, a magnificent hall and an imposing entrance. Also in 1889 Thomas Baker erected a covered approach way from his Royal Castle Hotel to his handsome new billiard and smoking rooms.

The Local Board was also involved in an important change. In 1888 it purchased an old farm near the Crown Hotel, and cleared most of the site, thus doing away with one of the last farms located in the centre of old Lynton. In the following year the Local Board converted an old barn it had left standing there into a market, which could be used by farmers bringing produce to sell in the village. On this site a new market building was to be built in 1901.

In 1889 Lynton began to expand westwards from its original core into the green meadows which lay along the valley floor. Houses were erected on both sides of Lee Lane (now Lee Road). Edward Pedder opened a new road across Bates Meadow. It was called 'Cross Street' because it provided the first connection between Lee Lane and Lydiate Lane. Mr Pedder was kept busy selling off building plots and before long houses began to spring up along his new road. 'The meadow is fast being built on and only a small portion is left for future disposal', the *North Devon Journal* announced in January 1890. Property developers were also busy at Lynmouth in 1889. John Heywood and Charles Medway were both busy erecting cottages and shops in the

A late-Victorian billhead. A wide range of services are listed. The name Church Hill has already been corrupted to Churchill, the name it bears today.

village. On the Tors Estate several villas were erected.

In the same year houses were being erected at Lynbridge. Land prices were lower further out of the resort and this encouraged the Lynton and Lynmouth Hotel and Property Company to begin constructing terraced dwellings there. These properties were intended to meet the increasing need for housing to accommodate the growing labour force.

So 1889 was a year of expansion with buildings rising up on all sides. Yet the rate of growth was soon to escalate still further. The new wave of development would far surpass all that had gone before.

A few words started the boom. When, at the opening of the Cliff Railway on Easter Monday 1890, George Newnes promised to give 'every assistance' to a pier project, he little realised the impact his words would have. Local businessmen were ecstatic. All too often in the past their hopes for a pier had been dashed, but they felt sure that Mr Newnes would succeed where others had failed. The opening of the cliff railway had provided ample proof that he had both the resolve and the financial resources to turn words into deeds. The *North Devon Journal* commented: 'Lyntonians have developed a healthy respect for the thoroughness which characterises Mr George Newnes M.P. in all that he says and does. If once he puts his hand to the plough, there will be no turning back'.

If further evidence was needed of Mr Newnes' commitment to build a pier, he

Lynton, c.1879. Many of these properties would be demolished and replaced by new ones in the building boom of 1887-1892.

Lynton in the mid-1880s. The hospital and Gordon Villas (now Victoria Lodge) are the only substantial properties yet built in the fields to the west of the village.

View of Lynton from Hollerday Hill, c.1888. The newly-built Kensington Hotel can be seen beyond the Church, but this is just before the building boom really gathered pace. Cross Street has yet to be started.

Maypole-dancing, c.1900. The view shows the western extent of Lynton at the time. Hollerday House can be seen on the hill.

soon provided it. In 1891 he applied to Parliament and obtained his Lynmouth Harbour Act. This Act dwarfed all previous proposals for piers at Lynmouth in both the scale and cost of the works proposed. It gave him the powers to extend the esplanade north-westwards 377 yards to give access to a solid pier, which would extend out 286 yards to the low-water mark. The sea bed was to be dredged so that vessels could come alongside the pier at most stages of the tide. This would enable excursion steamers to make the resort a regular port of call. It would also make it much easier for cargo vessels to bring in freight.

George Newnes' pier scheme ignited an explosive burst of building activity. Local businessmen were confident that once access by sea was improved they would grow rich by catering for a greatly increased number of visitors. They took part in an undignified scramble to acquire land and build on it. Many invested their life savings. Others borrowed heavily. Two new banks were opened to cope with the business. In little more than a year the face and character of Lynton and Lynmouth was changed for ever.

'New buildings are looming up in all directions,' declared the *Lynton and Lynmouth Recorder* in February 1891. 'Have you heard that in future building land at Lynton will be sold by the inch?' asked the same newspaper in May. The demand for land was forcing prices up to

Lynton, in the early twentieth century. Fox and Fowler's Bank stands on the corner and shops adjoin it. This block was built in 1891.

Queen Street in the early twentieth century. Much of this street had been rebuilt between 1890 and 1892. On the left is an old building, with steps leading up to it, which was nicknamed 'Rats' Castle'. It was demolished in 1911 and the Temperance Cafe was built on the site.

unprecedented levels. Those with land to sell could name their own price. Builders enjoyed a bonanza. It probably seemed as

if the whole resort was one gigantic building site.

In 1891 the centre of Lynton was altered almost beyond recognition. Old property was ripped down and replaced by new. Opposite the church, Mr Prideaux's old smithy was demolished, and work began to build a thirteen-bedroomed boarding house (Castle Hill House) and some shops. Next to these shops Fox and Fowler and Co. opened a substantial new bank. On Pig Hill a handsome new Post Office and a shop were erected. In Queen Street the old Globe Inn and the dilapidated cottages adjoining it were demolished. A new inn was opened on the site and next to it work began to construct two new shops. Much better access was provided to Queen

Street by the construction of a new road starting from the Royal Castle Hotel.

Following the opening of the Cliff Railway, Lee Lane was to become Lynton's new central axis, and as early as 1891 a few businesses began to seek sites along it. In April the Devon and Somerset Bank began transacting business from their new premises in a prime position facing the entrance to the Cliff Railway. By August work had begun on a new shop next to the bank.

Throughout 1891 houses were being erected in the fields to the west of old Lynton. New villas were springing up on both Lee Lane and Cross Street. The first house was built in Park Gardens.

Most important of all, George Newnes announced that he would be erecting his mansion on Hollerday Hill. Here was further proof of his long-term commitment to the resort. In May 1891 Jones Bros. began work to excavate an approach road to the site.

Down at Lynmouth substantial building works were also in progress. In November 1891 work began to erect a large lodging house in a field by the Watersmeet Road. By this time the Lynton and Lynmouth Hotel and Property Company had decided not to demolish the lime kilns. Instead they were busy pulling down some dilapidated old buildings by the esplanade, and beginning work to erect two large shops there. Six other shops were opened in Lynmouth in the course of that year. On the Tors estate a number of large villas were 'dropped in appropriate

Lynmouth, c.1900. The large buildings on the right were erected in 1892, The Mary *is being unloaded in the harbour.*

View across the East Lyn to Tors Road in the Edwardian era.

nooks' on the hillside, while down by the East Lyn over a dozen cottages were erected on the new Tors Road.

Opinions differed on whether this pell-mell development was for the better or worse. Most of the inhabitants saw it as an age of great progress, with the cliff railway, esplanade, electricity works, modern houses, shops and hotels all testifying to the enterprise of local men. Yet many visitors were horrified to see a rash of ugly buildings disfiguring the picturesque scenery. One national guide declared that it was: 'A sore offence to some who, in every ominous placard offering eligible building sites, foresee the day when their beloved solitude will be overwhelmed by bricks and stone'.

In February 1892 came news which punctured the bubble and left the inhabitants shocked and bewildered. George Newnes announced that he had decided to drop his pier scheme. Hopes were destroyed. Many faced financial ruin. Angry businessmen demanded an explanation.

At first Evan Jeune of the Manor House was blamed. The son of a former Bishop of Peterborough, he had spent many years in Australia, but in 1883 he had married Ada Medland Lock-Roe, the eldest daughter of the late Robert Roe, and had become the part-owner of the manor of Lynton. It was said that Mr Jeune had demanded £10,000 for the land required to erect the pier and related works, and this was why George Newnes had abandoned the scheme. For a time Evan Jeune was the most unpopular person in the resort.

The western limit of development at Lynton, c.1910.

A General Store on Orchard Terrace, c.1899. On the right is Miss Lucy Ridge who kept the shop.

Soon it became clear that Mr Jeune was not entirely to blame. He explained to the local press that, when the pier scheme had first been proposed, he had offered to lease all the land that Mr Newnes had originally asked for and had asked only a nominal rent of £2 per annum. He also pointed out that George Newnes had eventually decided on a much more elaborate scheme, and had obtained an Act which gave him the power to make a compulsory purchase of 22 acres of manor land. Mr Jeune had considered this to be far more land than was needed for the pier scheme and had suspected that George Newnes planned to build houses on some prime sites by the sea. He said

Lynmouth in the 1890s. Many of the houses had balconies overlooking the river.

Lynmouth after 1911. By this time some thought the village had been over-built.

this was why he had demanded £10,000 for the land. Mr Newnes had declared that he was not prepared to negotiate and had dropped the whole scheme.

For his part George Newnes stated that he was no longer prepared to spend £40,000 of his own money on a pier which he claimed would benefit the manor authorities far more than him. He felt that, because of his Act, the owners of the manor had already made huge profits from selling land at inflated prices, and he was not going to pay them large sums to buy their land.

There may well have been another reason why George Newnes had second thoughts about his pier scheme. Once he had decided to build a summer home in Lynton, his enthusiasm for improved landing facilities seemed to wane. It seems likely that he listened to other wealthy residents, and they convinced him that the resort's air of peaceful gentility would be badly damaged once crowds of day-trippers began to land at a pier.

George Newnes loved to be popular. Knowing how desperately the trades-people wanted a pier, he would not have wanted to attract their hostility by expressing this view in public. Secretly, he was probably relieved when his disagreement with Mr Jeune gave him a pretext for abandoning his scheme.

The collapse of the pier project had

Lynmouth, c.1900. On the left are the Bridge Buildings and then the Lyn Valley Hotel.

Lynmouth, 1907. Island Cottage is on the right.

Lynmouth, 1907, looking much as it did until the flood disaster of 1952.

Cottages at Middleham, c.1910. They were destroyed in the 1952 flood disaster.

serious repercussions. Property prices plummeted. Many who had speculated found that they had lost heavily. New shops and houses stood empty and had to be auctioned off at knockdown prices. It was the building industry which suffered most. One builder was bankrupted and others were obliged to lay off most of their workmen. In November 1892 the *Lynton and Lynmouth Recorder* reported: 'The consequence is that it has brought nearly all building operations to a standstill. Numbers of workpeople have had to leave and go to the Welsh side to obtain work, which has caused a great depression of trade in the neighbourhood'.

Census figures show the effects of the economic boom and the collapse that followed it. In the forty years between 1841 and 1881 the population of the parish had only increased by 186, rising from 1,027 to 1,213. However, in the next decade the population grew by 334, reaching 1,547 in 1891. Yet in the decade from 1891 to 1901 the population increased by only 94 to a figure of 1,641 in 1901.

The great boom had ended. Business confidence had been destroyed and it was to be many years before Lynton and Lynmouth again began to grow significantly.

The Coming of the Railway

THE first serious proposal for a railway to Lynton and Lynmouth had been put forward back in 1878. It had been followed by a whole series of other ambitious schemes. None of these had been conceived by Lyntonians, none of them had been planned with the resort's interest principally in mind, and nothing had come of any of them. The promoters had hoped to obtain the financial support of the big railway companies, but this had not been forthcoming. The Great Western Railway (GWR) and the London and South Western Railway (LSWR) had examined the schemes. They had decided that the district was too sparsely populated to offer any hope of a reasonable financial return on their investment, so they had refused to get involved.

Early in 1894 there was gloom in the resort. Hoteliers and lodging-house keepers had few advance bookings, builders had no work, working men were travelling to Wales looking for jobs. The prospect of another poor season led many local people to step up their demands for a pier, as the only way of improving trade.

By a strange irony it was this clamour for a pier which prompted a new attempt to obtain a railway. In June a crowded public meeting at the Foresters' Hall demanded that the Local Board should take steps to build a pier. Evan Jeune chaired this meeting and he was totally opposed to the idea. It seems likely that he feared it would lead to an influx of day-trippers. He certainly did all that he could to persuade the noisy audience that they would do better to support a railway. He pointed out that a pier would only be used in the summer months, whereas a railway would serve the resort all the year round. This, he claimed, would increase the number of wealthy residents. The meeting was not convinced. Speaker after speaker argued for a pier. Mr Jeune realised that he was losing the debate. To try to head off the pressure for a pier, he offered instead to try and interest one of the major railway companies in building a railway from Barnstaple. The meeting agreed, though they made it clear that their campaign for a pier would continue.

Evan Jeune became the principal player in the first moves to obtain a railway. Galvanised into action by his worries about a pier, he was soon busy sounding out the major railway companies and financial bodies to see if they would be willing to give backing to a railway scheme. He also asked Crawford Barlow, a railway engineer, to seek the support of George Newnes. Early in July Mr Barlow met George Newnes, who said that he

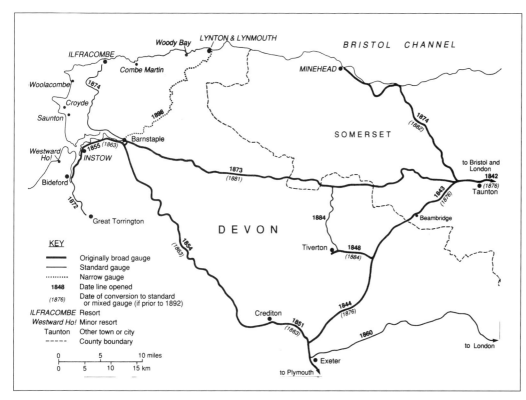

Railways serving the North Devon resorts in 1900.

would be willing to help, but only if the railway was a light one.

Mr Jeune soon had the backing not only of George Newnes, but also of Thomas Hewitt and William Halliday. By September these four local gentlemen had decided to promote a Bill in Parliament. They proposed a narrow-gauge railway connecting Lynton with the LSWR line at Barnstaple. In doing this they must have been well aware that, for any one travelling from distant parts, the slow, circuitous rail journey via Exeter and Barnstaple would place the resort out of reach for a day trip. It was also clear that the change of gauge at Barnstaple would prevent the through running of excursion trains. So these four leading members of the local gentry were proposing a line of a kind that would effectively prevent large incursions of rail-borne trippers. They also must have hoped that their scheme would

cause the inhabitants to forget their demands for a pier.

Then came a bombshell. On 18 October Crawford Barlow wrote to Mr Jeune advising him that Lord Fortescue, a major North-Devon landowner, was going to promote a rival Bill. Lord Fortescue's scheme proposed a standard-gauge railway from Lynton to Filleigh on the GWR's Taunton to Barnstaple line. It was backed by the GWR, who at last had been spurred into action by the fear that the LSWR might gain an advantage. This proposal would have provided a much shorter route from London and the Midlands. Through trains could have operated on it, as there would have been no break of gauge. This proposal alarmed the local gentry, for excursion trains would easily be able to run to Lynton if this railway was built.

Public meetings were held in Lynton so

Lynton, 17 September, 1895. A procession leaves the town on its way to the cutting of the first sod ceremony for the Lynton and Barnstaple Railway. Lady Newnes can be seen in the first carriage.

that the inhabitants could decide whether to support the Lynton and Barnstaple Railway Bill or Lord Fortescue's Lynton Railway Bill. Not surprisingly, large numbers attended. The people knew that a railway might bring the resort out of recession, so they wanted to make the right choice.

Some of the inhabitants secretly preferred many aspects of Lord Fortescue's proposal. They realised that it would provide a more direct link with the national rail network. Yet they suspected that his scheme was intended mainly for the benefit of his own estates. They also knew that in the past Lord Fortescue had been a leading sponsor of proposals for

railways to Lynton which, after promising much, had turned out to be nothing more than 'paper railways', not a single length of track ever having been laid.

Many locals were disappointed that the proposed Lynton and Barnstaple Railway would still cause travellers from most parts of the country to go on a long roundabout route to reach Barnstaple, and then would oblige them to change to a 'toy train' for the ride to Lynton. On the other hand, they knew that the Lynton and Barnstaple Railway had the backing of gentlemen who were genuinely interested in the resort. This convinced them that this railway stood a much better chance of actually being built. So the

The cutting of the first sod took place in a field where the Lynton Station was to be built. Lady Newnes holds a bouquet. George Newnes is the bearded man to her right. Lady Newnes used the silver spade to put the first sod into the oak barrow.

inhabitants voted to support the Lynton and Barnstaple Railway Bill and to oppose the Lynton Railway Bill. Both Bills went before a Select Committee of the House of Lords. On 26 March 1895, after sitting for seven days, the committee

A triumphal arch erected at the entrance to Lynton to celebrate the cutting of the first sod.

Another arch put up to celebrate the cutting of the first sod. This one is on the entrance road to Sir George's mansion. The house can be seen on the hill.

passed the Lynton and Barnstaple Railway Bill and threw out the Filleigh scheme.

Later that day a telegram arrived at Lynton. It simply said: 'We have got our Bill'. The people rejoiced. Cannons fired and a candlelit procession wound its way through the streets. The Lynton and Barnstaple Railway Bill then passed through the House of Commons without opposition and it received the Royal Assent on 27 June 1895.

Even then some Lyntonians wondered whether the railway would be built. They remembered only too well how George Newnes had obtained an Act to build a pier and then abandoned his plans. George Newnes, though, seemed anxious to make amends for previously having

disappointed so many people. He was probably keen to win back their affection and esteem. This time there was to be no change of mind. He became a leading financial backer of the railway, took on the chairmanship of the company and was soon making arrangements for the construction of the line.

On a sunny day in September 1895 an enthusiastic crowd gathered to watch the ceremony of 'cutting the first sod'. A field near the proposed Lynton terminus of the railway was the location for this happy occasion. Lady Newnes was given the honour of daintily digging a small hole with a silver spade. Afterwards Sir George jokingly declared that she had performed the task in such a workmanlike fashion that he was considering whether to 'give

Navvies laying the track for the Lynton and Barnstaple Railway in the Yeo valley near Barnstaple, c.1897.

her regular employment in the construction of the railway'.

Sadly this day of joyous celebration was to be followed by many months of frustration as disputes and practical problems bedevilled the construction of the line. Some landowners stood out for five times the value of their land. George Newnes described their demands as 'downright robbery'. This meant that work on the line only began in March 1896. Then progress was delayed by the nature of the terrain. The contractor was James Nuttall of Manchester and he soon found that his navvies were having to excavate far more cuttings through hills of solid rock than he had been led to expect.

There was also concern about the siting of the Lynton station. From the outset it had been made clear that the terminus of the line would be on a hill some 700 feet above sea level and well outside the village. George Newnes explained that this was because of the engineering difficulties involved in bringing it further down into Lynton, and also because he did not wish 'to disfigure the little Alpine villages'. While most Lyntonians were far from happy with such an inconvenient location, they eventually accepted the reasons for it. What they could not accept was that their Council was finding reasons for not honouring its promise to build a new road from the station to Lynton. This would mean that all carriages operating between Lynton and the station would have to negotiate the very steep Shambleway Hill (now Sinai Hill), or go a long way round via Lynbridge.

The railway was finally opened on 11

Arching the viaduct at Chelfham, c.1897. Timber was cut to size in the saw mill in the foreground.

May 1898. On nearing Lynton the official train stopped to allow Lady Newnes to cut some ribbons extended across the line. The train then wheezed into the station. Fog signals were set off. The excited crowd cheered and waved.

At long last Lynton had its own railway. The directors deserved the congratulations that were showered on them. They had dipped deeply into their pockets to provide a public service. It would not return them a penny-piece in dividends until 1913.

George Newnes soon cast a shadow over the celebrations. At a luncheon in the Valley of Rocks Hotel later that morning, he spoke in solemn terms of a recent proposal for a narrow-gauge railway between Minehead and Lynmouth. The promoters of this line were two Welsh railway companies. Their intention was to land excursionists from Wales at Minehead and then transport them by train to Lynmouth.

Sir George declared that he 'did not see why people who had built residential houses should be driven away by Cardiff speculators'. His hostility to the projected line was understandable. After all, in investing heavily in a railway which was impractical for day-trippers from distant parts to use, he had shown that he was determined to preserve the resort's exclusive character, even if it meant lower

Lynton Station, 7 March 1898. The first test run by a passenger train. The Taw *arrived with one coach. In the observation carriage are Evan Jeune and his wife, the lady of the manor. Contractor's debris is still lying about.*

Lynton Station, 9 March 1898. The Yeo *arrives with a party of reporters who had been invited to have a trial run. It was estimated that 300 people were at the station to greet the train.*

Another view of the reporters' train. Mr Jeune, in dark gloves, and Mrs Jeune, in dark hat and coat, can be seen standing by Yeo. *They entertained the press to lunch.*

Another trial train, this time shown after passing Collard Bridge in the Yeo valley. There were many bends on the route.

The formal opening of the Lynton and Barnstaple Railway at Barnstaple Town Station, 11 May, 1898. A large crowd has gathered. George Newnes can be seen in the centre. The tall man on his right is Thomas Hewitt.

Lynton, 11 May, 1898. The train has stopped just short of the station to allow Lady Newnes to cut red, white and blue ribbons. An excited crowd looks on.

Outside the Kensington Hotel at Lynton, May 1898. The last coach to Barnstaple is about to depart. It was no longer needed following the opening of the railway. Coaches still ran to other local towns.

profits for his company. Small wonder then that he should express his anger that others should threaten to destroy the resort's select social tone. He must also have been worried that this proposed railway would prove a serious competitor to his line. The proposed line to Minehead was intended to connect with the GWR's West Somerset Railway, so it would offer a much shorter route to Taunton and from there to London and the Midlands.

Sir George issued a stern warning. If the line from Minehead was built, he declared that he would never visit Lynton and Lynmouth again. He had chosen the best possible moment to give his warning, for this was the day celebrating not only the opening of his railway, but also the laying of the foundation stones for the Town Hall, and he was paying for that too.

The inhabitants were faced with a difficult dilemma. They realised that the proposed line from Minehead would provide a much more direct link with the major rail networks, and an opportunity to gain an important share of the Bristol Channel excursion trade. Yet most people felt they could not afford to upset their great benefactor.

In the following weeks the promoters of the proposed railway from Minehead canvassed support in the area, but it was only in Lynmouth that they received any backing at all. A few Lynmouth businessmen signed the petition, because they believed that the proposed railway would

A station horse-bus waits to meet a train at Lynton Station, c.1900.

particularly benefit their village. They also feared that the new line from Barnstaple was channelling tourists into Lynton to the detriment of Lynmouth. Lynton was solidly against the proposed railway, even though the resort was being given its best-ever chance of becoming more easily accessible from distant parts.

At a public enquiry held at Minehead in August, the Lynton gentry expressed their concern about influxes of vulgar Welsh trippers. Exmoor landowners also objected because they claimed the proposed line would interfere with stag-hunting. Their combined opposition proved decisive and the whole plan was dropped.

Once again it had proved to be George Newnes, backed by a few other wealthy residents, who had determined the way in which Lynton and Lynmouth should

develop, by preventing it from being invaded by large numbers of trippers.

So Lynton and Lynmouth had to make do with an attractive but impractical railway. In the early days local pride caused many to ignore its limitations. Yet praise soon turned to criticism as the problems became all too apparent. Passengers, already wearied by a long journey, had to face delays and inconvenience when they changed trains at Barnstaple. Then there was the slowness of the journey: an hour and three quarters to cover nineteen miles. No wonder one reporter declared: 'A hearse would have done it in less time!' The difficulties were not at an end when the Lynton terminus was finally reached, for horse-drawn transport had to be used to complete the journey from the out-of-town station.

Lynton Station, c.1904. The train is collecting wagons from the goods shed. Stationmaster Robert Fursdon stands on the platform.

Passengers board the train at Lynton Station, c.1905. Engines reversed on their return to Barnstaple as there was no turntable at Lynton.

Travel on this line was undoubtedly a novel experience. Tourists loved the 'toy train' and admired the scenery they passed on their journey to Lynton. Yet the rural nature of the country the train passed through was to be its downfall. The whole area was too sparsely populated to support a railway. The fact that the line did not pass through the main villages *en route* was also a disadvantage. Outside the

main holiday season, the railway always ran at a loss. With the advent of the motor vehicle, competition rapidly increased. The LSWR took over the line in 1923, but the improvements they made to both track and rolling stock could not prevent heavy financial losses.

Sadly, in 1935 it was announced that the railway would have to close. A meeting was held in Barnstaple to hear the views of objectors, but the arguments of protesters from Lynton and Lynmouth were weakened when it became apparent that many of them had travelled there by car! Once closed the railway would be remembered with nostalgia. Some would dream of a day when the line might be reopened, so that once again steam engines might puff into the little station at Lynton.

Pressure for a Pier

WHEN in 1894 Evan Jeune, George Newnes and Thomas Hewitt announced their intention to provide Lynton and Lynmouth with a rail link, they hoped that this would cause the business community to drop its campaign for a pier. They were to be disappointed. Pressure for a pier persisted.

Arguments for and against a pier split the resort, dividing Lynton from Lynmouth, businessmen from wealthy residents, conservationists from developers. Never had there been an issue which provoked such bitter arguments. The strength of feeling was not surprising, for this was an era when there was an enormous increase in the Bristol Channel passenger steamer traffic. Many people wanted to obtain a bigger share of that profitable excursion trade. Others feared that if a pier was built, the resort would become a tripper's paradise and its character would be permanently changed.

In June 1894 Bob Jones attended a meeting of the Local Board. He explained that at a recent public meeting the ratepayers had made it very clear that they desperately wanted a pier and that he had been asked to represent their views to the Board. Mr Jones told the Board Members that, if they agreed to have the esplanade extended to a point nearer deep water, he had reason to believe that 'a company would undertake to construct a solid pier to below low-water mark at spring tides'.

The majority of Board Members were themselves businessmen wanting a pier and they were persuaded by Bob Jones' argument. A small minority, led by Evan Jeune, were totally opposed to the idea of spending public money on a pier. The business faction easily won the vote and plans for an extension to the esplanade were drawn up.

In June 1895 the new Lynton Urban District Council awarded Jones Bros. the contract to construct a 1,100-feet extension to the esplanade at a cost of £3,000. Work was soon in progress digging and blasting out the face of the cliff. The stone was used to build a massive sea-wall. Even those opposed to the scheme had to admit that it provided employment for a substantial number of local men in a period when jobs were short and many went hungry.

Shortly after work on the esplanade commenced, the Urban District Council received two rival offers from business interests prepared to build and manage a pier. A Mr Pickivell of Cardiff said that he was prepared to construct a 700-feet open-ironwork pier out to a concrete head, and to run it as a private venture. Jones Bros. of Lynton offered to build a

Lynmouth, c.1889. The second part of the esplanade has still to be built. The cutting for the cliff railway is still incomplete.

similar pier and likewise operate it as a private business. Both parties said that the Council would be given an option to purchase the pier they built for £25,000.

Those members of the Council who had backed the move to extend the esplanade were delighted when they heard the news, for it seemed to vindicate their decision to risk so much of the ratepayers' money. Their initial enthusiasm was dampened when they realised that both offers had strings attached. Mr Pickivell required a subsidy of £200 a year once his pier was opened. Jones Bros. wanted the Council to guarantee to pay them a £300 subsidy in any year in which the profits from the pier did not reach £150.

After agonising over the issue the Council members finally decided that they could not agree to give subsidies to a private pier company. Complaints were already coming in thick and fast about the use of ratepayers' money to build the esplanade extension. The Council decided it would have to wait for a private company that would offer to build a pier without any further financial help from the Council. No company came forward, for there were grave doubts about the financial viability of a pier at Lynmouth.

So the new part of the esplanade was opened in June 1896, still without any prospect that a pier would actually be built. At the opening ceremony the speeches referred in glowing terms to the advantages of having a pleasant promenade for visitors to stroll on. Yet everyone knew that the real reason why the esplanade had been built was to act as a starting point for a pier. It was already

Woody Bay Pier, c.1898. Opened in 1897, it had only a short life. After being badly damaged by storms, it was demolished in 1902.

looking as if it would be a very expensive 'white elephant'.

In December 1896 Evan Jeune and Captain Walter Hume resigned their seats on the Council in protest at the sums they felt had been squandered on the esplanade. It is significant that, on a council dominated by tradespeople, these were the only two members who had come from the ranks of the local gentry.

In February 1897 came news which rocked the resort. The *North Devon Journal* reported: 'A communication has been received from Messrs P.A. Campbell Ltd to the effect that they intend landing steamers at Woody Bay instead of Lynmouth next season'. The business community's worst fears seemed to be realised. They knew that Colonel Lake, a property speculator, was trying to create a new resort at Woody Bay and that as part of his scheme he was having a pier built. They feared that Lynmouth would lose its steamer trade to Woody Bay.

Public meetings were called at which worried businessmen once again pressed for a pier to be built at Lynmouth. Fortunately for them, the steamer company relented and decided to continue calling at Lynmouth.

Then in the summer of 1898 came even more surprising news. Evan Jeune, who only recently had been bitterly opposed to all pier schemes, announced that he was actually backing a new pier scheme. What was more, it was proposed that this pier should be to the east of the Lyn at Blacklands Beach on his estate, instead of starting from the end of new esplanade extension.

Lynmouth, 1919. The resort still lacks a pier and passengers still have to be ferried out to the steamers. The flags suggest that this is either a regatta or lifeboat day.

What were the reasons for Evan Jeune's change of mind? Was it the fact that he was to receive a rental of £20 a year for a lease on the land, 250 shares in the company and the chance to become a director? This hardly seemed sufficient incentive for such a dramatic shift in his attitude. Had he suddenly been persuaded of the need for a pier by the local businessmen? It hardly seems likely. Was it that he had decided to become only an occasional visitor to Lynton and Lynmouth, and so was more interested in the profits that might be made from a rise in land values, than by the need to preserve the resort's high social tone? Or was his real motive an urge to make a point to the Council which had rejected his advice and had spent so heavily on the esplanade extension? At this distance in time it is impossible to know. What is certain is that the proposal caused a sensation.

This pier was to be principally financed by business interests in South Wales. It was to start from a point some 300 yards east of the manor house and would be 1,200 feet long. Steamers would be able to come alongside at any state of the tide. The pier was to be built on piles and there was to be space at the end for a pavilion and a bandstand.

Parliamentary powers were obtained to build the pier. Yet the scheme was abandoned in 1900, because of strong opposition from George Newnes, Thomas Hewitt and other members of the local gentry.

Still the pier issue raged on. In the

Artist's impression of the pier that was proposed in 1898.

summer of 1901 the local press devoted countless pages to the debate. Newspapers took sides. The *North Devon Herald* argued the gentry's case declaring that if the resort built a pier they would be opting for 'the pence and impudence of the holiday tripper' who sought only 'Punch and Judy shows, shooting galleries, Aunt Sallies and switchbacks', but what would be lost would be 'the fat cheques and the crisp bank-notes of the better-class families' who summered there every year. The *North Devon Journal* took the opposite view and argued that the man who could only afford a day's holiday was equally entitled to visit the resort, and the idea that only 'undesirables' would come by steamer was an insult to working men.

The Lynton Council spent countless hours discussing the issue. Yet, despite all the huffing and puffing, nothing was done, largely because financiers could not be persuaded to risk their capital when they could see that the people of influence living in the resort were so strongly opposed to it.

If a pier had been built the character of the twin villages would have changed for ever. Perhaps we have much to thank the Lynton gentry for. They ensured that Lynton and Lynmouth remained a small, picturesque resort rather than a large, commercialised one.

Shipwrecks and Lifeboats

THE Bristol Channel was one of the busiest waterways in the world. Great ships left Bristol and the South Wales ports for foreign destinations. Small coastal craft traded between the many small harbours on the Welsh and English coasts. Fishing boats operated in the inshore waters. Inevitably a certain number of these vessels became casualties due to bad weather or navigational errors.

While Bideford Bay had the worst reputation as the graveyard of ships, the rocky coast near Lynmouth also had its quota of wrecks. From time to time a vessel would be disabled in a storm. Then it would be swept helplessly by wind and tide, to find its last resting place at the foot of Foreland Point or in one of the nearby bays.

As early as 1792 there is a record of a tempest which dashed a vessel up on the rock-strewn shore below the Valley of Rocks. Local men risked their lives scrambling down the cliffs. They found not a single person alive, only one corpse thrown up on the rocks. For a week they toiled, bringing salvaged goods to the top of the cliff. The 7s. 6d. they each received hardly seemed a fair reward for their efforts.

On the night of 20 January 1820 there was a violent gale, accompanied by a blizzard. The West Indiaman *Picton*, outward-bound from Bristol, was driven ashore in Lynmouth Bay. Not until the next morning did the wind abate sufficiently to allow attempts at rescue. Most of the crew and a lady passenger were saved after being lashed to the mast and rigging for many hours. Unfortunately the cook and a boy had frozen to death. On the same night the sloop *Thetis* struck a rock off Lynmouth while sailing from Bristol to Ilfracombe. Two lady passengers were drowned when a boat capsized while trying to reach the shore.

A dramatic rescue took place in February 1855. One stormy morning a vessel in distress was sighted out in Lynmouth Bay. A 240-ton West-Africa trader *Victory* of Bristol was being blown by a westerly gale towards Foreland Point. Her two masts had snapped off and four human beings could be seen lashed to their stumps. Huge waves were rolling over the stricken vessel as the wind and tide swept her ever closer to the cliffs.

At that time Lynmouth had no lifeboat, but it did have an extremely brave coastguard lieutenant. On the morning of the storm Lieutenant Hodges was sick with a fever. Yet, when he was told about the stricken vessel, he rose from his bed, put on his uniform and hurried to the harbour where a small crowd had gathered. He called for a crew. Eight men stepped forward.

Without a thought for their safety, the lieutenant and his crew rowed out of the

Looking down on Lynmouth in 1854. At this time many sailing vessels and steamships used the Bristol Channel. Summerhouse Hill derived its name from the summer-house on the left.

harbour. The boat pitched and rolled as it was buffeted by huge waves. Often it was lost to sight as it sank into the trough of great rollers, sometimes it was nearly swamped by walls of foaming water, but eventually it returned with the four nearly dead survivors, two men, one woman and a boy. Cheers rang round the harbour for those who had risked their lives to save the lives of strangers.

On 22 August 1868 a hurricane blew a much larger vessel into the bay. This was the 800-ton sailing ship *Home* of St Andrews, New Brunswick. This vessel had left Bristol in ballast for Canada where it was due to collect a cargo of timber. Its masts had snapped off and it was drifting helplessly before the wind, dragging its anchor. A boat was launched from the ship and four men reached the shore. Then attempts were made to lower the ship's lifeboat, with one man in it to attend to the ropes. As the boat hit the sea it broke loose and was swept onto the rocks. The unfortunate seaman was drowned. The ship's longboat was then lowered and ten members of the crew made it to the shore.

Four men and a boy were left on board waiting for death as the ship drifted helplessly towards the rocks. Miraculously, at the last possible moment, the anchor held. At first light one of the men tried to swim ashore with a rope, only to drown in the raging seas. Later that morning the gale abated sufficiently for a Lynmouth crew to be able to put out in a coastguard boat and rescue those still on board.

This was an occasion when two of Lynton and Lynmouth's most controversial characters were seen in a much more favourable light. Robert Roe risked his life on Countisbury Foreland, helping to save some of the shipwrecked mariners. He was awarded a silver medal by the Royal National Life-boat Institution for his gallant conduct. The R.N.L.I. also sent 10 guineas to be shared among the seven Lynmouth men who had assisted him.

Following this rescue the Revd Lawson began raising funds to set up a lifeboat station at Lynmouth. He collected £25 during a church service. Then he went round the local gentry asking for donations. It was the Revd Lawson who wrote a letter to the *Times*, pointing out that the nearest lifeboat was stationed at Ilfracombe and appealing for financial help. As a result of this letter an anony-

Lynmouth in c.1865. The lifeboat house has yet to be built.

mous benefactor offered to provide a boat for Lynmouth.

A boat-house was needed to house the lifeboat. Robert Roe generously offered to provide a site. He became president and the Revd Lawson chairman of the committee formed to find the £200 required to cover building costs. The efforts to raise funds for a lifeboat house were redoubled in September of that year after a Barnstaple smack foundered near Foreland Point. The crew were rescued, but only with great difficulty.

Before work had even begun on the boat-house, Lynmouth heard in January 1869 that the new lifeboat was on its way from the builders, Messrs Forrest of Limehouse.

Quite remarkably it was brought overland. On 20 January 1869 it arrived by train at Barnstaple station. It was originally intended that it should do the remainder of the journey by sea, but the people of Lynton and Lynmouth wanted to have the honour of launching their first lifeboat. So it was brought by road, being dragged by a team of 11 horses all the way from Barnstaple. As the boat was 30 feet long and 7½ feet wide, the task of negotiating the narrow lanes was very difficult. Particular care had to be exercised when descending Lynmouth Hill.

On the following day Mrs Roe performed the official naming and launching ceremony. It was announced that the £400 cost of the ten-oared lifeboat had been met by a Yorkshire lady in memory of her brother and would be called the *Henry*. It was temporarily housed in a shed on the beach.

In the following month came the tragic news that one of Mr Roe's vessels, the *Topsy*, had foundered off Minehead. After leaving Newport with a cargo of coal for Lynmouth, it had run into a ferocious gale. Rolling heavily under bare masts, it

Mrs Roe names Lynmouth's first lifeboat Henry *in January 1869. The crew wait for the launching so they can try out their new vessel.*

had suddenly sunk. All four on board had been drowned. The dead were the master, two seamen and a small boy, who was being given a passage home. A fund was set up to care for the destitute wives and children of the lost seamen. Many local gentlemen gave generously.

This tragedy encouraged more donations for the lifeboat house. The building was finally completed in March 1870. Above it was a public reading room. It had been paid for and well-stocked with books by the local gentry. They obviously thought that the provision of reading facilities for the sailors and working men of the resort was another good cause that deserved their support.

Strangely, once the lifeboat had arrived, the elements seemed to relent and only twice was the *Henry* called out on a mercy mission. The lifeboat's first rescue took place on 28 June 1871 when a packet boat was in trouble in the bay. This small boat had just been purchased for landing passengers and goods from the packet steamers. Earlier that morning it had been towed from Ilfracombe. It had arrived at low tide, so William Groves, the only man on board, had had to drop anchor and

wait out in the bay. Without warning a gale blew up and he found himself in great danger. The *Henry* was launched and William Groves was saved. The crew were rewarded with a meal at Rock House given by Mrs Whitehead.

Not until 19 March 1876 was the *Henry* again called on. This time it was the schooner *Lizzie Morton* of St Ives which was in trouble. Bound from Penarth in South Wales for Par in Cornwall with a cargo of coal, the schooner had lost her masts in a sudden squall. It was drifting helplessly towards the dangerous rocks at Highveer Point near Heddon's Mouth. After rowing hard for 1½ hours the lifeboat reached the schooner and rescued the crew, hauling them through the waves by breeches buoy.

In 1887 the R.N.L.I. decided that the time had come to replace the *Henry*. In April of that year the *Louisa* arrived by sea from Minehead. She was a larger boat, being 34 feet long. She again had ten oars. This lifeboat was to have a much more eventful career, playing a major part in the saving of 11 vessels and 39 lives.

It was on 12 January 1899 that the *Louisa* was involved in an epic rescue which was to win both lifeboat and crew lasting fame. A tremendous gale had blown all day and the sea was raging. Huge waves were breaking over the sea wall, flooding houses and a shop. At 7.52 p.m. Jack Crocombe, the Lynmouth coxswain, received a telegram from Porlock Weir stating that a large ship was drifting ashore there and was sending up distress signals. Soon afterwards another telegram was received from Watchet stating that they were unable to launch their lifeboat because of the severe weather. This meant that Lynmouth was the only lifeboat station within reach of

Lynmouth in the 1890s. The lifeboat house is the second building along the riverside. Steps lead up to the reading room. The triumphal arch in front of the Bath Hotel indicates that this photograph was taken on a special day.

the stricken vessel. The crew was summoned and quickly assembled. It was soon apparent that it would be impossible to launch the lifeboat at Lynmouth, in the teeth of such a ferocious gale.

Desperate moments demand desperate measures. The crew of the stricken vessel needed help and the men of Lynmouth would not let them down. Jack Crocombe announced that they would take the lifeboat overland to Porlock. Many in the small crowd of onlookers gasped in disbelief, for they knew that the proposed journey was 13 miles long. It would mean climbing to a height of 1,423 feet above sea level. It would also involve coping with gradients of 1 in 4½ while ascending Countisbury Hill and gradients of 1 in 4

while descending Porlock Hill. Nevertheless many men and women volunteered to help. Some twenty horses were brought down from the stables of Tom Jones, the coach proprietor at Lynton.

A dozen horses were harnessed to the lifeboat and the journey began. Half a dozen men were sent ahead with pickaxes and shovels to dig down the banks and widen the road. Oil lamps and flares were used to light the road.

Problems soon developed. Some of the horses were frisky and would not pull properly. The lifeboat and its carriage together weighed about ten tons and it seemed as if it would be impossible to haul it up Countisbury Hill. Yet with the

Fishermen mending their nets at Lynmouth in the 1890s. The lifeboat crew usually included several local boatmen.

assistance of some hundred locals the summit was eventually reached. Here there was a delay when a wheel came off, the lynch pin having been loosened by continual banging against the bank. Eventually it was put back and they set off again.

Now the going got really tough. Lashed by incessant rain and battered by the gale, most of the helpers decided to turn back. Only about 20 remained to help the lifeboat crew.

A serious difficulty lay ahead. On reaching the section of road known as Ashton Lane they realised that it was barely wide enough to allow the lifeboat through, let alone the carriage. It would be quite impossible to widen the road

sufficiently. Some began to lose heart but not Coxswain Crocombe.

'We've come so far and we're not going to turn back!' he declared. He had some of his men take the lifeboat off its carriage and put it on skids, so that it could be dragged along the narrow road. Others pulled down gate posts to allow the carriage to go through onto the moor. Eventually boat and carriage were reunited and the journey continued.

Going down Porlock Hill was especially hazardous, for this was one of the heaviest loads ever to have made the steep descent. Every man heaved on drag ropes to help the horses hold the carriage back.

At the bottom of the hill was another

Lifeboat day at Lynmouth in the Edwardian era. A band leads the lifeboat men along the street towards the Louisa.

obstacle. A garden wall blocked the way. The old lady who lived there was very angry to be woken in the early hours by the sound of demolition work on her property. Yet once she realised that a ship was in danger she dropped her objections and could not have been more helpful. She even allowed a corner of her cottage to be knocked down to allow the carriage wheels through.

The lifeboat men turned at last onto the road that led to the coast, only to find that a sea wall had washed away in the storm and part of the route was impassable. After diverting onto a higher road and felling a large tree which blocked their way, they finally reached Porlock Weir at

6.30 a.m. They were exhausted, soaked to the skin and hungry.

Yet, without pausing to rest or eat, they immediately launched the lifeboat. The crippled ship had drifted eastwards and it took almost an hour to reach her. She was perilously close to Hurlstone Point. Her anchors were just holding and keeping her off the dangerous rocks.

The *Forrest Hall* was a full-rigged sailing vessel with a crew of 13 men and five apprentices. Early the previous day this 1,900-ton ship had left Bristol for Liverpool. The strong north-westerly wind had made sailing down the Bristol Channel difficult, so the master had asked a steam tug to tow her on the first stage of the

The crew of the lifeboat in the Edwardian era.

journey. The wind had risen to a gale and the towing cable had snapped. Then the master had ordered sails to be raised so the ship could be steered. Unfortunately, just as he gave the order, a great wave had smashed into the wallowing ship carrying away her rudder. Helpless, she had been blown towards the Exmoor coast. Her two anchors had been dropped but had dragged along the sea-bed. Then, by some miracle, the anchors had finally caught hold, just as she was about to go onto the rocks at Hurlstone Point.

The lifeboat crew hailed the *Forrest Hall* and were told that she was safe while the anchors held, but that most of the men and boys on board were shaken, seasick and exhausted from the terrible battering the ship had taken. The lifeboat stood by until daylight.

Just as dawn was breaking a tug steamed into the bay. It was the *Jane Jolliffe*, the tug from which the ship had parted company the previous day. The lifeboat managed to get a tow-line from the tug to the ship. Then some of the lifeboat crew went on board the *Forrest Hall* to help raise the anchors, for the ship's crew were too weak to do the job on their own. These were hazardous moments, for the gale was raging with

renewed force. Any mistake on the part of the tug would have seen the ship washed onto the rocks.

Slowly but surely the tug pulled the vessel away from immediate danger. Then it set course for Barry with the lifeboat escorting in case the tow-line broke again. It was a difficult journey, for the ship could not steer itself and the gale was whipping up huge waves. For a time the tug was unable to prevent her charge drifting close to the dangerous waters of Nash Sands. A second tug was signalled for and at last they were able to make better progress towards the Welsh coast. Darkness had fallen before the lifeboat finally accompanied the *Forrest Hall* into Barry. Only then did the crew realise how tired and hungry they were.

The following day the *Louisa* was towed most of the way back to Lynmouth by a steamship outward bound for Genoa. The crew had left as humble men simply doing their duty; they returned as heroes for they had taken part in the most famous lifeboat launch of all time.

Who were the crew members who took part in this celebrated rescue? They were Jack Crocombe (coxswain), George Richards (second coxswain), Richard Ridler (bowman), Richard Moore (signalman), Richard Burgess, Charles Crick, David Crocombe, William Jarvis, Bertram Pennicott, Thomas Pugsley, George Rawle, John Ridler, John Ward and 16-year-old William Richards. Edward Pedder, the owner of the Lynmouth Post Office where the telegram had been received, also sailed in the boat.

The *Louisa* became famous and many visitors admired her. The *Forrest Hall* rescue had been her finest hour; only once afterwards was she called into service. Vessels no longer needed assistance so

The new lighthouse at Foreland Point and the men who built it, 1900.

frequently. In part this was due to the steady decline in the number of sailing vessels.

The opening of a lighthouse on Foreland Point in September 1900 also helped to make navigation safer on this stretch of the Bristol Channel. This major engineering feat was carried out by the Lynton firm of Jones Bros. So difficult was the operation that some of the building materials had to be raised up the cliffs from the shore, using a lift working on a principle somewhat similar to that of the cliff railway.

Sadly, the time came when it was necessary to replace the *Louisa* with a more up-to-date lifeboat. In August 1906 she was taken by sea to Minehead and then by rail to London 'to be disposed of'. Her successor, the *Prichard Frederick Gainer*, was to remain in service until the Lynmouth lifeboat station was closed in 1944. This lifeboat took part in a number of important rescues, but none so eventful as the overland launch of the *Louisa* in 1899.

The crew practising in the Prichard Frederick Gainer *at Lynmouth.*

Recreations

'WITH such a scene before me, how poor in comparison seem the gaieties of the town,' declared John Swete in 1789. Picturesque scenery was certainly a lure for the first visitors to Lynton and Lynmouth. Those who sought man-made attractions had to look elsewhere. The resort was much too small to provide the assembly rooms, circulating libraries and theatres found in larger watering places. Yet, while early Lynton and Lynmouth lacked the artificial pleasures that enlivened life at more commercialised resorts, it did have some very special natural attractions.

The superb countryside surrounding the twin villages had much to offer. Guidebooks were packed with information about local beauty spots. Painting

Lynmouth, c.1828. Artists found the surrounding scenery had many attractions.

The New Inn at Lynmouth in 1847. Anglers found excellent river fishing. Salmon and trout were plentiful in the East Lyn.

and sketching were favourite pastimes. Remote coves and wooded combes beckoned for those who loved exploring. Salmon and trout abounded in the rivers for those who wanted to try their hand at fishing. Countless gulls could be shot on local cliffs, and there were boat trips to take you there.

The resort also offered opportunities to join the chase after the wild red deer. As early as 1808, the Valley of Rocks Hotel was advertising that excellent hunting was available in the vicinity. In 1857 a directory declared: 'A pack of staghounds is kept at Lynbridge, for the purpose of hunting the red deer of Exmoor Forest. They commence hunting in August and afford ample sport for the resident gentry and visitors'.

The hotels were always busy in the autumn stag-hunting season. The county gentry booked in and so did keen huntsmen from distant parts of the country. Town dwellers also welcomed the chance to share in the pageantry and excitement of an ancient country ritual.

'Stag-hunting is a noble sport,' declared one writer. It could also be extremely cruel. Often the deer was pulled down in full flight by the hounds. Sometimes it

A meet outside the Town Hall in 1907. Hunting was always popular with local farmers as well as the gentry.

Lynmouth in the early 1840s. The fact that Henry Trix's establishment is clearly shown on the right of this print may in part be explained by the fact that his library was the place where topographical prints were sold.

stood at bay only to be defeated by superior numbers. Occasionally the despairing beast swam out into the Bristol Channel. Even then there was no escape, for boats were sent out after it and it would be towed back to meet its death on the beach.

To see and be seen; that was the main aim of some Regency visitors. The 'quality' wanted to parade their beauty or the latest fashions. They also wanted to take the air and to admire the views. To meet these needs all genteel resorts were expected to provide a public walk. At Lynton it was Mr Sanford who in 1817 generously paid for a broad path to be cut along the cliff face. Known as North Walk, it led from Lynton out to the Valley of Rocks. Here the rich and famous sauntered each day.

By 1838 Henry Trix had opened a small circulating library next to the harbour at Lynmouth. Visitors could pay a subscription which entitled them to borrow the latest novels. Topographical prints and other souvenirs were on sale here. At his premises visitors could also have a sea-water bath.

'There is nothing to see there but respectability,' complained a travel writer after a visit to Lynton and Lynmouth in 1863. Yet this was precisely the quality that many Victorian tourists found so attractive. Some might criticise the resort for being dull, but many felt secure there because they were protected from brash and vulgar commercialised entertainment.

Fern-collecting was a typical example of the staid recreations favoured by mid-Victorian visitors. It was Charlotte Chanter, wife of an Ilfracombe clergyman and sister of Charles Kingsley, who first called attention to the many ferns that grew in the vicinity. Her book *Ferny Combes* was published in 1856. It described the ferns she had found on a tour from Lynmouth to Clovelly. Readers were advised to search for ferns while on holiday in the area. She claimed that it would provide 'innocent amusement and their restoration to health'.

Fern-collecting became a craze at Lynton and Lynmouth. Victorian visitors began to use the resort as a base from which to scour the countryside for rare specimens. Ferns were ripped out of the woods and hedgerows, to be replanted in pots in urban homes. Charlotte Chanter could not have realised that so many people would take up the hobby. She must have been dismayed at the pillage she had inspired.

Edmund Gill, a Lynton shoe-maker, decided to change his occupation and cash in on this wave of interest. He opened the Fernery on Lydiate Lane, supplying plants to those unable to find their own. By 1870 he was advertising

A family group outside Rock House, c.1865. Rock House was often let for the summer to wealthy visitors.

An 1870 advertisement for Edmund Gill's Fernery.

Croquet on the lawn outside Rock House, c.1865.

himself as an 'experienced collector' who could 'supply any quantity at one shilling a dozen and upwards'. He too was depleting the stocks of already rare ferns.

Fern-collecting must have seemed a trifle tedious to those accustomed to the 'high jinks' in fun fairs and music halls at commercialised seaside resorts such as Blackpool and Margate. Lynton and Lynmouth was a very quiet, sedate resort in the mid-Victorian era. The genteel game of croquet enjoyed mild popularity, but there was little to appeal to those seeking a lively lifestyle. In 1877 one bored visitor noted that the arrival of the steamers was the highlight of the day:

As there is no parade, no pier, and no band at Lynmouth, it is amusing to see what swelldom is reduced to by way of substitute. A cargo of oak timber sticks, deposited on the beach, served while I was there as the dais of fashion. Enthroned upon the sticks, surrounded by their admiring male attendants, some of the lady visitors contrived to improvise an 'upper circle' while awaiting the two events of the day,

These late-Victorian ladies sitting near the Tower may have been waiting for the steamer to arrive.

the arrival of the boat from Ilfracombe and the arrival of the boat from Portishead.

In such a quiet resort, the annual processions of the friendly societies provided a welcome diversion and always attracted crowds of spectators. The Society of Good Fellowship had been founded back in 1786. Its headquarters was at the Club House opposite the church and its parade was in June. The Lynton Branch of the Ancient Order of Foresters was only established in 1870. The Foresters' Hall, built in 1878, became its base. Its procession was in August.

A band often led the way on these annual friendly-society parades. Banners were carried and the members followed

behind. The procession wound its way through the main streets and then arrived at a hotel for lunch. Womenfolk and children joined in for the afternoon festivities.

The Lynton Band was certainly in existence as early as 1868. It was a brass band and the performers were mainly local tradesmen. This group often performed at local functions, but the musicians were not thought to be sufficiently accomplished to play for the visitors. In fact the band folded in the early 1870s, due to lack of support, but was reformed in 1876.

By 1882 Edward Hodges, a baker, had become the band-master, and, with him in charge, the standard of the Lynton Band

The Lynton Band leads the Society of Good Fellowship through the streets, c.1887.

The Society of Good Fellowship outside the Lyndale Hotel, c.1890. Some bandsmen can be seen on the right.

The Foresters' Hall.

greatly improved. Now the band began to perform for the visitors. Every summer it played regularly by the harbour. Its only income was the money the collector could badger out of those who listened.

Listening to music was a favourite Victorian recreation, and holiday-makers had come to expect a good quality band at the seaside. German bands were very much in fashion. Ilfracombe had long had one, but Lynton and Lynmouth had never been able to afford the services of a professional group. However, in 1890 the resort was booming and the business community decided that the time had

come to emulate their prosperous neighbour. A band committee was set up and enquiries were made.

A Herr Hahn offered to bring his nine-man string band from Bath for the summer months, if he was guaranteed £50 for the summer season and was allowed to collect freely in the resort. The Cliff Railway Company and eight leading hotels promised £3 each and the rest was raised from lodging-houses. The Rhine Band proved a great attraction. For many years it arrived by steamer for the summer season, 'as regularly as the swallows'. It performed on the esplanade at Lynmouth, opposite Churchill House at Lynton and outside all the leading hotels.

By this time Lynton and Lynmouth was at last beginning to offer its visitors a little more entertainment. There were, for example, several summer events which always pulled in the crowds. The annual lifeboat day was particularly popular. Hundreds would watch the procession through Lynmouth, followed by a ceremonial launching and then a demonstration of rescue techniques. Then there was the annual regatta. The programme included sailing and rowing competitions, swimming races, slithering along the greasy pole, and live duck-hunts.

The Working Men's Industrial Fair and Exmoor Pony Show was first held in August 1903. It, too, became an important occasion in the social calendar. The Industrial Fair was organised by local workmen, to raise funds for the Cottage Hospital. The Exmoor Pony Show was intended to heighten interest in the breeding of pure Exmoor ponies. This was something that Frank Newnes was keenly interested in and he became the president of the Pony Show. With such illustrious

The Lynton Band, c.1888. Edward Hodges, the bandmaster, is in the centre. His son Herbert is the drummer boy.

Lynton, May 1900. Processions were always popular. This one was to celebrate the relief of Mafeking. Coastguards carry the flags. Councillors, lifeboat men and the Lynton band lead the procession and school children bring up the rear.

Regatta Day, 1898. Flags are flying on the smack Mary. *Some spectators would arrive and leave on the steamers.*

Regatta Day, September 1899. Sir George Newnes was a judge. There may well be a greasy pole sticking out from the ketch Little Jane.

The Working Men's Industrial Fair and Exmoor Pony Show taking place in a field next to the Hospital, August 1909.

patronage the success of the combined event was guaranteed. Farmers, country gentry, townsfolk and visitors all mingled there and large sums were raised for the hospital.

The ladies' bathing-place on the west beach, c.1879. A bathing machine is waiting to bring the bathers out of the sea.

Attitudes towards sea-bathing had changed by the end of the nineteenth century. People no longer placed such faith in the curative properties of sea water. Now they were not prepared to put up with the ordeal of being dipped under the waves by an attendant. Instead they wanted to enjoy the novel experience of actually swimming in the sea.

For many years the main bathing-place had been just to the west of the lime kilns. When the esplanade extension was opened in 1896 it had steps running down to a small patch of sand, and this became the main bathing-place. The locals claimed that the sands here were growing, but one visitor declared that a microscope would be needed to detect any increase. Perhaps she had just stubbed her toe on a rock.

The main bathing-place was strictly reserved for ladies, for sea-bathing was segregated at Lynmouth, as elsewhere on the English coast. Men and boys were barred from bathing there between 8 a.m and 6 p.m. They had to trek to Wringcliff Bay, Blacklands Beach or Sillery Sands if they wanted to go in the sea. A bye-law of 1884 stipulated that no male bather over the age of ten years was permitted to approach within a hundred yards of the area set aside for female bathers, and that no female bather of any age was to approach nearer than a hundred yards to a male bather over the age of ten. Such rules separated husband and wife, mother and son, sister and brother, all in the cause of public decency!

Ladies were expected to use the bathing

LYNTON AND LYNMOUTH.

THE Crown Prince of Siam and attendants have been staying for a few days at Lynton, where they have occupied rooms at the Royal Castle Hotel.

E. B. JEUNE, Esq., J.P., of the Manor House, Lynmouth, met with an unfortunate accident at the opening run of the Devon and Somerset Staghounds. Whilst riding across the common his horse tripped in a bog, throwing its rider, who sustained a broken collar-bone.

ON Sunday afternoon last an address were given to the Wesleyan Sunday School by Mr. Lowe, of Birmingham, and in the evening the Rev. J. Beadle, a Bible Christian minister, conducted the service, delivering a very able and interesting sermon to a good congregation.

MR. E. HARLING, organist of the Parish Church, gave an organ recital on Thursday evening last, in aid of the choir and organist fund. The instrumental programme was interpersed with vocal solos, which were well rendered by Miss F. Hodges and Mr. C. Hewitt.

BATHING at Lynmouth this season has been more popular than ever before, as is evidenced by the large numbers which may be seen enjoying their dip every morning and evening. Considerable dissatisfaction is, however, felt at the restriction confining the hours available for gentlemen to bath before eight a.m. and after six p.m. It is thought, considering that the majority of bathers are of the sterner sex, an extra hour in the morning and evening would not be too much to expect. The subject is one which deserves the attention of all interested in the prosperity of the place, as many visitors are, through the present restriction, either debarred from bathing at all or have to put up with a long walk to other available places.

A news cutting of August 1899. Male bathers were already becoming dissatisfied with the arrangements made for them.

Bathing in front of the esplanade, c.1920. Mixed bathing had been allowed since 1907. Bathing huts have replaced bathing machines.

machines. By the 1870s there were several lined up on the beach. After the occupant had changed, the attendant was required to ensure that the machine was taken into a sufficient depth of water as would 'prevent any indecent exposure of such

The Greenhouse Tea Room in the Edwardian era.

person, when set down from such machine'.

By the beginning of the twentieth century many visitors were beginning to demand changes to the antiquated bye-laws. In 1896 Paignton on the South Devon coast had become one of the first English seaside resorts to permit mixed bathing. Several other Devon watering places were quick to follow. There seemed no reason why they shouldn't. Male nude bathing was a thing of the past. Resorts allowing mixed bathing always stipulated that males must wear neck-to-knee costumes.

Yet at Lynmouth the shackles of Victorian prudery were slow to slacken. As late as 1906 the Council took a stern stance when a few daring men and women began swimming together at the main bathing place. It declared that 'improper bathing' would not be allowed. A police constable was instructed to patrol the esplanade and stop the practice. The Council even extended the time that males were banned, by resolving that 'men and boys over the age of nine should be prohibited from bathing there between 8 a.m. and 8 p.m.'. Many considered this to

Lynmouth beach in the Edwardian era. Bucket and spade holidays had come into fashion.

Outing to Lee Bay, c.1910.

be 'silly legislation'. They argued that 'any party of decently-clad persons should be able to bathe together'.

The Council faced mounting opposition. In 1907 it had to give way and allow the sexes to bathe together. This proved

*Fishing at the turn of the century. A man prepares to net a salmon that the angler has caught. Ladies watch
from the balcony of Island Cottage.*

extremely popular. The *North Devon
Herald* was soon reporting: 'The number
of ladies and gentlemen indulging in a
swim has greatly increased'.

Once the sexes were bathing together,
the days of the bathing machine were
numbered. There was no longer any point
in concealing the ladies before they
entered the sea. It was only while
changing that privacy was required. So
bathing machines were soon replaced by
bathing tents down on the beach and by
bathing huts on the esplanade.

Visitors were now seeking pleasure
rather than improvement. They no longer
spent so long on serious pursuits such as
fern collecting and sketching. Children

were encouraged to play on the beach.
Parents could relax and enjoy themselves.

Outdoor recreational opportunities
multiplied at the turn of the century.
Steamer trips set off each day to Clovelly,
Lundy, Woody Bay and other attractive
destinations. In the summer of 1901 a
pierrot troupe began performing twice a
day on the esplanade at Lynmouth.
Cricket was popular. Only occasional
matches had been played after the club
had been formed in 1874, but now games
were played on a much more regular
basis. Golf flourished, first at Martinhoe
Common and then on the new links at
Caffins.

Indoor entertainment was also increas-

Hockey players outside the cricket pavilion in the Valley of Rocks, c.1919.

ing. At the Town Hall in September 1901, for example, performances were put on by a light-opera company and by a group of glee singers. There too, in the same month, a biograph show was proudly presented. The novelty of seeing moving pictures drew large audiences. Balls and private parties were organised in the larger houses for the local gentry and those visitors who were considered socially acceptable. Life was very pleasant for those with money and time at their disposal.

The otter hounds meet outside Cecil Bevan's Lyn Valley Hotel, May 1908. It was later reported that there had been a 'good day's sport but no kill'.

Motor Cars and Charabancs

IT WAS in July 1901 that the motor vehicle first arrived in Lynton and Lynmouth. A motor car owned by a nephew of Mr Tonge of Glen Lyn completed the twenty-mile journey from Minehead to Lynmouth in an hour and 25 minutes, a remarkably good time considering the nature of the gradients and the rough state of the road.

In 1902 more cars began to make the hazardous journey along the steep roads to Lynton and Lynmouth. They caused a sensation. Wide-eyed boys gathered to watch them; horses reared up and bolted.

In April 1903 Sir George Newnes astonished many residents when he arrived in a motor car. This was the man who had recently invested his money in a railway to the resort and here he was seemingly championing the new rival

The old and the new in Edwardian Lynmouth: horse-drawn carriages and an early motor car are present on the esplanade.

form of transport. Yet those close to Sir George were not surprised. They knew that he loved progress and always liked to be associated with anything new. They were also aware that, as a major shareholder in a French car-manufacturing firm, he had a vested interest in motor cars as well as in his railway.

In May 1903 Sir George surprised even more people when he inaugurated a motor-coach service from Ilfracombe to Blackmoor Gate Station. Once again he was leading the way. This was the first time in England that motor buses had been run to provide a feeder service to a railway.

So why had Sir George decided to promote the motor coach? After the opening of his Lynton and Barnstaple Railway he had expected that visitors from Ilfracombe to Lynton and Lynmouth would travel by horse-drawn coach as far

as Blackmoor Gate and then would complete the journey by train. His hopes had not not been realised. Most people had found it both quicker and pleasanter to complete the whole journey on the four-horse coach, rather than having to change at Blackmoor Gate. Sir George now hoped that the speed and novelty of a motor-coach service to Blackmoor Gate would persuade most people to use it, and this would result in his trains being busy between Blackmoor Gate and Lynton.

It was a good scheme but it failed. In July the driver of one of Sir George's two motor buses was fined by Combe Martin Magistrates for 'driving a motor bus at a speed greater than 8 miles per hour'. Sir George was furious. He knew that many cars already travelled at much greater speeds and he thought his bus service was being discriminated against. He closed the service. The two motor coaches were sold

THE . . .
ROYAL CASTLE HOTEL,
LYNTON.

The LEADING HOTEL, standing in its own Grounds of 9 acres, facing the Sea. Lighted throughout by Electricity.

Motor Garage.
Pratt's Motor Spirit.

Telegraphic Address—
" Castle, Lynton."

A postcard of c.1910. Hotels were quick to recognise that they had to provide facilities for motorists.

Outside the Royal Castle Hotel at the time of the coronation of King George V in June 1911. The hotel displays an AA sign and has a garage.

to the GWR, who used them on a feeder service between Helston and the Lizard.

The number of motor cars arriving in Lynton and Lynmouth rapidly increased. Over the Easter weekend in 1906 almost 60 cars visited the resort. By the summer of that year the Royal Castle Hotel, Tors Hotel, Lyndale Hotel and Lyn Valley Hotel had all opened garages for their customers' cars and were providing much-needed repair facilities.

Early motor cars were not equipped to descend the steep hills leading to Lynton and Lynmouth. All too often there were reports of brakes overheating and cars crashing. Countisbury Hill soon gained the unenviable reputation of being the most dangerous hill in the country and many cars met an undignified end on it.

Lynmouth Hill was another dangerous hill which had its share of accidents. Climbing the hills was almost as big a problem and breakdowns were frequent. The Cliff Railway began to do a brisk business transporting cars between Lynmouth and Lynton.

In 1903 some residents campaigned to have motor cars banned from Countisbury Hill. One letter to the press declared: 'Motor cars, like traction engines and railway engines, are all very well in their proper place but that place is not on our narrow roads'. Such letters were inspired in part by concern at the number of crashes. Yet it also seems that not everyone in Lynton and Lynmouth welcomed the advent of the motor vehicle. Some saw the motor car as a

One of the many early cars that crashed on Countisbury Hill.

hustling, bustling intruder threatening the leisured calm that Lynton and Lynmouth had long been famous for.

In response to this campaign, the Barnstaple Rural District Council in November 1903 proposed prohibiting all motor vehicles on Countisbury Hill. The hoteliers of Lynton and Lynmouth protested loudly, for they feared losing most of the wealthy motorists who were patronising their hotels. The Council backed down and the road remained open.

The accidents continued. Action was needed, so in November 1906 the Barnstaple Rural District Council decided to play its part in the building of a new motor road from Minehead to Lynton and Lynmouth. The route was to be via Dunster, Exford and Simonsbath. It would make it possible for motorists to avoid both Countisbury Hill and Porlock Hill.

Cars eventually began running along the new road, but dangers still faced unwary drivers. Between Combe Park and Barbrook vehicles had to negotiate the notorious Beggars Roost, which was even steeper than Countisbury Hill. Cars had grave difficulty climbing this hill and several ran away descending it. In June 1912 there was a fatal car crash on this hill. Soon afterwards the Lynton Urban District Council decided to construct a new road over Lyn Down so that motorists could avoid the hill. When this road and the new Station Road were completed after the First World War, they provided a much better access route to Lynton.

Local businesses had to adapt. Garages steadily replaced stables at the principal

An early car being taken up the Cliff Railway, c.1903. The tracks in the foreground enabled carriages to be easily removed when freight or cars had to be loaded.

hotels and large houses. The Cross Street works of Elliott and Gamon, which had built splendid carriages, became Elliott's Garage and now built and repaired motor cars. In 1910 Prideaux's Garage opened next to the Hospital and provided a chauffeur-driven car-hire service for those who previously would have hired a horse-drawn carriage.

In the years immediately before the First World War some small motor coaches known as charabancs also began to arrive at Lynton and Lynmouth. These vehicles were becoming a popular way of going on a short summer excursion to the resort, for they were open-topped and gave people a chance to try motor travel at relatively low fares. A few of the horse-drawn coach excursions from nearby towns began to be withdrawn as more and more people switched to the quicker charabancs. The Lynton and Barnstaple Railway also began to suffer the effects of this new competition. In 1912 the railway company blamed a fall in its receipts to the 'constant increase in charabancs'.

Lynton and Lynmouth was slow to adopt this new form of public transport. In 1914 Jones's coach office was still advertising trips in horse-drawn vehicles to Simonsbath, Hunter's Inn, the Doone

A motor car climbing Beggars Roost, c.1908. This steep hill was considered the ultimate test.

*A badly damaged car on Beggars Roost.
This may have been the vehicle involved
in a fatal accident in 1912.*

Valley and other local beauty spots, in addition to their four-horsed coach service to Minehead. Yet even in Lynton and Lynmouth there were signs of change. In 1914 a Mr Attree applied for a licence to run a charabanc service between Lynmouth and Watersmeet. Eighty-two people signed a petition against it on the grounds that the narrow road would become unsafe for walkers and horse-drawn traffic. Despite these objections the Lynton Council decided that it could not stand in the face of progress and granted the application.

Charabancs were ideal for short trips, but it was the arrival of a few much larger motor coaches on long distance excursions which heralded an even more

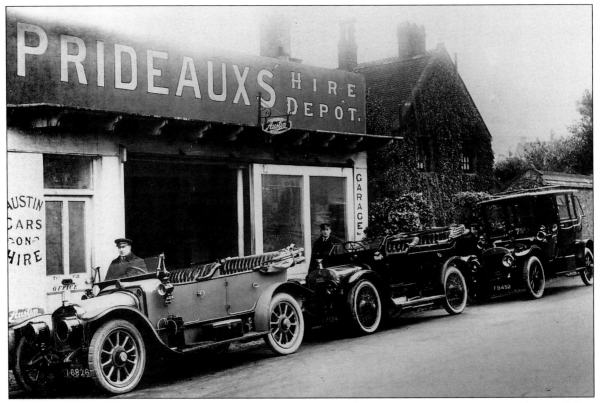

*Prideaux's Garage, Lee Road, Lynton, c.1920. It offered a chauffeur-driven car-hire service. Robert Ralph
stands by the middle car. In 1910 he had been sent to Lynton to start the business by Mr Prideaux, a
Barnstaple garage proprietor.*

significant change. In July 1912 a motor bus owned by Bristol Tramways brought a group of railway workers to spend a night at the Royal Castle Hotel. The local press reported that this was 'the largest motor vehicle yet seen in Lynton'. What seemed more surprising to some residents was that a group of men who earned their living in a goods-yard could actually afford to travel to Lynton and stay a night in one of the town's leading hotels. In the years that followed many more motor coaches would bring a growing number of working-class visitors from distant towns.

After the First World War the pace of change quickened. The last horse-drawn coach service between Ilfracombe and Lynton and Lynmouth was soon withdrawn. In March 1920 came the announcement that the famous 'four-in-hand' coach service to Minehead was to close. The *North Devon Journal* declared that this was no time for sentiment, pointing out that Hardy's new motor coaches would do the journey between Minehead and Lynmouth in two hours as compared with the three hours and a half taken on the horse-drawn coach. It also tried to reassure readers with the news that the new motor buses would keep on the famous old coaching names *Lorna Doone* and *Red Deer*. This was scant comfort to those tourists who had loved to start their holiday with a ride on the horse-drawn coach.

It was not only some for the visitors who mourned the passing of the horse-drawn coach. Ostlers, coachmen and

Setting off down Lynmouth Hill, c.1920. Robert Ralph is the driver.

blacksmiths all lost their jobs and many horses had to be slaughtered. For a few years more the horse-drawn coach was still used on trips to the Doone Valley, but nothing could stop the rapid increase in motor vehicles. Travel to Lynton and Lynmouth was becoming faster and cheaper than ever before.

*   *   *

Looking back some eighty years, it is clear that the outbreak of the First World War marked the end of an era. Yet it was not apparent at the time. The initial reaction was an outburst of patriotic fervour rather than concern at the threat to the tourist trade. Hotheads threw stones at the hotels where German waiters were employed and Thomas Hewitt gave half a crown to men who enlisted to fight for their country. The mood became more sombre as these young Lyntonians began to leave for the front. It also became clear that life would not be easy for those who stayed behind. Hotels and lodging-houses emptied out as their visitors hurriedly left for home.

Peace returned in 1918, but sadly most of the wealthy residents and richer visitors did not come back. They had frequented Lynton and Lynmouth for so many years, but now they preferred to seek out more exclusive watering places overseas, for they realised that the motor vehicle was at last opening up the resort to a new class of visitor and it was no longer the select retreat they had loved. Slowly the large houses they had occupied were sold off and were turned into boarding houses and private hotels.

Changing forms of transport at Lynton in the 1920s. A charabanc, car, bicycle, horse and rider and two coaches can all be seen.

The Lynton and Lynmouth Volunteer Training Corps drilling in February 1915. Many younger or more able-bodied men were already overseas fighting for their country.

masses. In doing so they made certain that the resort would remain small and would keep its scenic beauty. We have much to thank them for. An air of quiet tranquillity is present, even now. Walking past the many Victorian buildings, or strolling along cliff-side paths, it is easy to imagine stepping back in time. Lynton and Lynmouth has not changed as much as most other seaside resorts and this is its special charm.

Yet, though most of the gentry have long since gone, they have left a lasting legacy. By preventing a pier being built, and by ensuring that Lynton and Lynmouth was served only by a 'toy railway', they managed to exclude the

Suggested Reading

To put the resort of Lynton and Lynmouth into its county context see John F.Travis's *The Rise of the Devon Seaside Resorts, 1750-1900* (1993).

For the national context refer to John K.Walton's *The English Seaside Resort: A Social History, 1750-1914* (1983).

For the early history of Lynton and Lynmouth see John F.Chanter's *History of the Parishes of Lynton and Countisbury* (1907).

Also of interest, if you can find a copy, is T.H.Cooper's *A Guide Containing a Short Historical Sketch of Lynton and Lynmouth* (1853).

For a colourful account of life in Lynton and Lynmouth in the 1850s see W.H.Thornton's *Reminiscences and Reflections of an Old West-country Clergyman* (1897 and 1899), 2 vols.

Smuggling is given excellent coverage in a book which proved extremely helpful in writing a chapter of this book: Graham Smith, *Smuggling in the Bristol Channel, 1750-1850* (1989).

Lifeboat history is detailed in Grahame Farr's *Wreck and Rescue in the Bristol Channel: The Story of the English Lifeboats* (1966).

The history of members of the Geen family is outlined in M.S. Geen's *An Ordinary Devon Family: Geen of Okehampton* (1975).

Those interested in an attempt to create a rival resort in a nearby bay should see Harriet Bridle's *Woody Bay* (1991).

Index

agriculture 8, 20, 45, 46, 48, 66, 67
Albert Edward, Prince of Wales 67
Americans 63
Appledore 41, 42
artists 15, 161-62
Attree, Mr 181

Bailey, Charles 47-48
Bailey, Charles Frederick 92, 117
Baker, Thomas 66-69, 77, 92, 121
bands 72, 74, 77, 104, 165, 166-68, 169
banks 124, 125, 126
Barbrook 8, 24, 78, 80, 179
Barbrook Mission Chapel 83
Barbrook National School 83-84
Barbrook Orphanage 83-84
Barbrook Wesleyan Chapel 79, 80, 83
Barbrook Wesleyan School 79, 80, 81, 83
Barlow, Crawford 134-35
Barnstaple 8, 13, 17, 18, 23, 24, 25, 27, 30, 67,
    94, 135, 136, 143, 144, 145, 146, 154
Barry 159
Bath 18, 33, 34, 64, 168
Bath Hotel 110, 113, 156
bath-house 65, 88-89, 90, 91, 113, 164
bathing 58, 88, 171-74
bathing machines 57, 88, 89, 171-72, 174
Beach House 113
Beggars Roost 179, 181
Bevan, Mrs 63
Bevan, William 55, 119
Bideford 33
Blacklands Beach 149, 171
Blackmoor Gate 177
Blackmore R.D. 62-63
blacksmiths 68, 125, 183
bowls 105
Brendon 40, 49, 53
Bridgwater 29
Bristol 8, 12, 13, 32, 33, 34, 35, 38, 90, 152,
    158

building industry 19-20, 52, 119-33
businessmen 35, 51, 112, 114, 115, 118, 119,
    124, 130, 147, 149, 150

Caffins 174
Campbell, Revd R.J. 103
Castle Hill House 125
Castle Hotel 25, 30, 31, 32, 62, 66, 67, 92,
    105, 121, 126, 178, 182
Chanter, Charlotte 164
charabancs see motor coaches
Cherrybridge 92
cholera 90
churches 75, 78, 83, 87 see also individual
    churches
Churchill House 121, 122, 168
cinema 175
Clarke, Dr John 48, 67, 76, 92
Cliff Railway 99, 108-116, 119, 122, 126,
    127, 168, 178
climate 88
Clooneavin 19, 50, 64
Clovelly 174
coaches 23-31, 33, 49, 65, 67, 68, 144, 177,
    180, 182, 183, 184
coastguards 41-42, 153, 169
Coleridge, Samuel Taylor 16
Collard, William 79
Collins, Charles 79
Colwill, Sam 26
Combe Martin 85, 177
Combe Park 24, 79, 179
Comers, Mary 80
commons 45-49
Congregational Chapel 76, 79, 102
Congregational Church 103
Continent (of Europe) 13, 14
Convent 86, 87
Cooper, Dr Thomas 44, 62, 88, 90
Cornwall 33, 38, 70, 155
Cottage Hospital 92-94, 123, 168

Countisbury 23, 29, 42, 53, 63, 64, 65
Countisbury Hill 23, 30, 156, 178, 179
Cowell, Dr William 62
Cox, Revd Walter Eustace 85, 87
Cremorne, Lady 64
cricket 100, 174, 175
Crocombe, Jack 155-59
Croft Place 79-80
Crook, John 92, 119
croquet 165
Cross Street 121, 123, 126
Crown Hotel 17, 62, 76, 100, 121
cutting of the first sod 136, 137, 138-39

death-rates 95
Dibdin, Charles 23
Doone Valley 180, 183
Doyle, Sir Arthur Conan 104
Dulverton 30

Electric Light Company 117-18, 127
Elliott's Garage 180
Elworthy, Mrs 65
enclosure 45-50
esplanade 52, 108, 111-12, 114, 115, 124, 126, 127, 147-49, 150, 168, 171, 174
excursionists 34-36, 71-72, 113, 116, 124, 134, 135, 140, 144, 145, 147, 151
Exeter 8, 10, 23, 27, 54, 60, 63, 77, 135
Exmoor 8, 15, 25, 37, 60, 61, 63, 64, 66, 70, 145, 162

farmers 8, 41, 43, 45, 46, 48, 66, 81, 92, 121
    see also agriculture
ferns 84, 99, 164-65, 174
Filleigh 100, 135, 138
First World War 183, 184
fishing 50, 64, 117, 162, 174
fishing industry 8, 10-13, 24, 38, 66, 157
flood 8-10, 120, 132
Foreland Point 40, 152, 153, 160
Foresters' Hall 100, 134, 166, 168
Forrest Hall 158-59
Fortescue, Lord 135
Fotte, Mr 19
France 13, 14, 17, 38
friendly societies 166-67

gas 117-18
Geen, Charles 117
Geen, Thomas 52-59
gentry 35-36, 47, 64, 135, 145, 149, 150-51, 153, 162, 175, 184
Gill, Edmund 164-65
Glen Lyn 19, 108, 114, 176
Glenthorne 39-40, 53, 64, 65, 117
Globe Hotel 17, 43, 44, 125
golf 100, 174
Gordon Villas 101, 123
Greenhouse Tea Room 172
Groves, William 155

Halliday, Revd Walter S. 19, 40, 50, 53-55, 57, 59, 64, 117
Halliday, William 135
Hahn, Herr 168
harbour 8-11, 24, 37, 51-59, 108, 124, 153, 164
health 88-95
Heath, Angel 64
Heddon's Mouth 40
Herries, Robert 19
Heywood, John 109-15, 121
Hewitt, Copley 72, 74
Hewitt, Fanny 70-71, 73-74
Hewitt, Peter 71, 72, 74
Hewitt, Thomas 69-74, 98, 107, 109-14, 135, 143, 147, 150, 183
Hill, Daniel 17
Hodges, Edward 166, 169
Hodges, Lieutenant 152
Hoe 70-71, 73, 74, 98
Hollerday Hill 95, 98-99, 100, 104, 106, 126
Hollerday House 95, 98-99, 100, 104, 105, 106, 107, 124, 126, 130, 137
Hollier, Henrietta 65
Holman, John 119
hotels 17, 19, 22, 92, 118, 127, 162, 168, 183
    see also individual names
Hume, Captain Walter 149
Hunter, Major Patrick 68, 108
Hunters Inn 180
hunting 50, 64, 67, 145, 162-63, 175
Huxtable, Richard 80

Ilfracombe 8, 25, 26, 30, 32, 33, 34, 35, 36, 38, 39, 41, 58, 90, 152, 153, 166, 168, 177
inhabitants 45, 50, 88, 91, 94, 119, 127, 135, 136, 137, 144
inns *see* hotels
Ireland 38
iron ore 64
Island Cottage 63, 65, 131, 174

Jeune, Ada Medland 101, 127, 141, 142
Jeune, Evan 127, 129-30, 134-35, 141, 142, 147, 149-50
jetty 9-11, 51, 53, 54, 55, 89
Johnson, Ursula 62
Jones, Bob 101, 102-03, 110, 114, 147
Jones Bros. 98, 101, 114, 116, 126, 147-48, 160
Jones, Tom 27, 71, 156
Jones, Miss 119
Jones's Coach Office 27, 180
Jose, Giles 68
Jupe, Isaiah 79, 85

Kekewich, Revd Charles 76
Kensington Boarding House 119, 123, 144
Knight, Frederic 64, 66
Knight, John 24-25, 61
Knight, Hon. Mrs 61

lace-making 73, 74
Ladywell 92
Lake, Colonel B. 149
landowners 92, 135, 145
Lane, Mary 78
Lawson, Revd William 69, 75-85, 87, 153-54
Lean, Father Hugh 87
Lean, James 92
Lee Abbey 47, 48, 92, 117-18
Lee Bay 173
Lee Road 82, 86, 87, 92, 101, 103, 106, 121, 126
libraries 155, 161, 164
lifeboat house 154, 155, 156
lifeboat men 72, 169
lifeboats 153-60, 168
lighthouse 160
lime kilns 8, 9, 51, 52, 53, 114, 115, 126, 171

Litson, John 91
Litson, William 13, 17
Local Board 67, 68, 91, 92, 94-95, 100, 110, 111-12, 114, 117-18, 134, 147
Lock, John 18, 23, 45-47, 48, 51, 66
Lock, Mary 48-49
Lock, William 11, 45
lodging-houses 17, 19, 20, 24, 94, 126, 168, 183
London 33, 34, 71, 103, 135, 144
Lorna Doone 62
Lundy 38, 174
Lydiate Lane 24, 76, 121, 164
Lyn Valley Hotel 119, 131, 178
Lynbridge 8, 74, 101-02, 114, 122, 139, 162
Lyndale Hotel 20, 21, 22, 30, 89, 119, 120, 167, 178
Lynmouth Free Church of England Church 78, 83
Lynmouth Free Church of England School 78, 80, 81, 82
Lynmouth Hill 24, 108, 154, 178
Lynton and Lynmouth Hotel and Property Company 115, 119, 122, 126
Lynton British School 79-80, 81, 85
Lynton Cottage 18, 46, 47, 69
Lynton National School 52, 61-62, 67, 76, 77, 78, 80-82, 83, 85
Lynton Wesleyan Chapel 82, 83
Lynton Wesleyan Church 82, 93

manor 10-11, 18, 23, 45-50, 51-59, 119, 130
manor house 53, 98, 127, 150
market 121
Mars Hill 24, 64, 92
Martin, Thomas 41
Martinhoe Common 100, 174
Maton, William 15-16
Medway, Charles 68, 121
Midlands 33, 34, 144
Middleham 83, 117, 132, 135
Minehead 8, 29, 30, 31, 36, 67, 100, 140, 144, 145, 154, 155, 176, 179, 181
Mortlock, John 76
motor cars 31, 97, 98, 146, 176-80, 182, 183, 184
motor coaches 177-78, 180-82, 184

Mundy, Matthew 60-63, 64, 66

Nautilus 56, 66
Nelson's Cottage 64
New Inn 11, 12, 22, 162
Newnes, Frank 97, 104, 106, 107, 168
Newnes, George 95, 96-107, 113-14, 122, 124, 126, 127, 129-30, 134-35, 137, 138, 139, 143, 144, 147, 150, 170, 176-77
Newnes, Priscilla 96, 98, 101, 104, 106, 107, 136, 137, 138, 140, 143
Newport 154
Nonconformist chapel 76, 80
North Walk 70, 74, 111, 114, 115, 164
Nuttall, James 139

Okehampton 117
Orchard Terrace 129

packhorses 8, 10, 41, 42, 49, 52, 66, 108
Parish School 83
Park Gardens 126
Parracombe 65
parsonages 20, 60-61, 78
Pedder, Edward 121, 159
Pickivell, R. 147-48
pier schemes 36, 57-59, 71, 99, 108, 111-12, 113, 114, 116, 119, 122, 124, 127, 129-30, 132-33, 138, 147-51
piers 33, 35-36, 116, 134, 135, 165, 184
pierrots 174
Pig Hill 125
Plymouth 8
Plymouth Brethren chapel 78
poets 16-17
population 8, 19, 133
Porlock 13, 29, 41, 42, 156
Porlock Hill 156, 157, 179
Porlock Weir 155, 158
Portishead 33-34, 113, 166
Post Office 125
Prideaux, Thomas 68, 125
Prideaux's Garage 180, 182
Prospect House 20, 87

Queen Street 44, 125
Queen's Hotel 119

railways 25, 27, 29, 30, 31, 33, 34, 71, 99, 101, 104, 113, 134-45, 177, 180
Ralph, Robert 182
rates, ratepayers 24, 90, 92, 100, 112, 147, 148
Rawdon, General J.D. 50, 64, 89
recreations 161-75
regattas 168, 170
reredos controversy 77-78
revel 43-44
Rhenish Tower 51, 90, 166
Riddell, William 77, 108, 114
Ridge, Mrs 84
roads 8, 17, 20, 22, 23-31, 37, 49-50, 108, 126
Rock House 78, 83, 155, 164
Rock Lodge 108
Roe, John Colwell 49, 52
Roe, Mrs 154, 155
Roe, Revd Thomas 48-49, 64
Roe, Robert 49, 53-59, 92, 127, 153-54
Royal Castle Hotel, *see* Castle Hotel

sailing vessels 8, 32, 51, 56, 152-53, 154-55, 158-59
St John the Baptist Church, Lynmouth 78, 79
St Mary the Virgin Church, Lynton 9, 13, 43, 49, 61, 62, 65, 67, 75, 76, 123
Sanford, Mary 64
Sanford, William Ashford 18-19, 23, 46, 47, 163
scenery 14-17, 19, 58, 127, 161, 184
schools 68, 75, 76, 78-85, 87 *see also* individual schools
Scott, Revd John James 24
Selwyn, Mrs 25
sewerage 90, 91-92
Sharp, John 67
Shelley, Percy Bysshe 17
shipwrecks 65, 66, 152-55
shops 118, 121, 125, 126, 127
Short, John 10-11
Sillery Sands 171
Simonsbath 25, 66, 179, 180
Sinai Hill 76, 94, 95, 102, 139
Six Acre 48
Skinner, Revd John 23

smuggling 37-42
Somerset 18, 23
South Molton 60
Southey, Robert 16-17
steamers 32-36, 55, 108, 112-13, 116, 124,
    149, 150, 165-66, 170, 174
stocks 49, 68
stone circles 16, 46
Sullivan, Michael 42
Summerhouse Hill 153
Summit Castle 20, 78, 105
Swansea 32, 34, 90, 105
Swete, Revd John 15, 23, 161

Taunton 27, 30, 144
Tenterden, Lord 117
Thornton, William Henry 63-66
Tit-Bits 96-98, 102
Tiverton 30
Tonge, Mr 176
Topsy 154
Tors estate 119, 122, 126
Tors Hotel 119, 120, 178
Tors Road 127
Town Hall 72, 82, 100-02, 104, 144, 163, 175
trade 8, 10, 56
Trentishoe 41
Trix, Henry 90, 163, 164
Trix, Mrs 65

Urban District Council 95, 100, 101, 147-48,
    151

Valley of Rocks 15-17, 45-49, 100, 152, 164,
    175
Valley of Rocks Hotel 17-18, 25, 30, 45-46,
    48, 49, 53, 75, 92, 115, 116, 119, 121, 140
Veall, Richard 79
Vellacott, Nathaniel 43
Vestry meetings 24, 76, 90
visitors 14-22, 27, 30, 32, 33, 34, 35-36, 42,
    45-46, 48, 63, 90, 124, 145, 151, 183

Wales 8, 17, 18, 32, 34, 35, 51, 105, 133, 134,
    140, 150, 152, 155
water mills 8, 101-02
water supply 90, 92, 94-95, 107

Watersmeet 24, 49-50, 181
Watersmeet Road 126
Whitehead, Mr 78
Whitehead, Mrs 78, 82, 83, 85, 155
Woody Bay 149, 174
woollen industry 13, 17
Wordsworth, William 16
Working Men's Industrial Fair 168, 170
wrestling 43-44
Wringcliff Bay 60, 171